1/2008

475th Fighter Group

Aviation Elite Units • 23

OSPREY
PUBLISHING

475th Fighter Group

John Stanaway

Series editor Tony Holmes

Front Cover

In mid-October 1943, New Guinea-based USAAF and RAAF bomber and attack aircraft commenced an aerial offensive against the Japanese stronghold of Rabaul. In turn, Imperial Japanese Navy aircraft targeted Allied shipping in nearby Oro Bay, and it fell to V Fighter Command units to protect these vessels. In the vanguard of the defence was the P-38 Lightning-equipped 475th FG.

At 0930 hrs on 17 October, the group's 431st FS was scrambled from Number 12 airstrip when 15-20 A6M 'Zekes' were intercepted by the 432nd FS over Oro Bay upon their return from a mission to Lae. Amongst the pilots to engage the enemy was leading group ace, 1Lt Tom McGuire (in P-38H-5 42-66836). His combat report from the mission read as follows;

'We were ordered off by the controller and sent to Tufi at 0930 hrs, after which we were told to proceed to "angels 20" over Oro Bay. I was leading "Hades White Flight". We were at 23,000 ft when we sighted the enemy at a position of "eleven o'clock", slightly above us (a group of from 10-20 Zeros). After we dropped our belly tanks, 1Lt Kirby, in his capacity as squadron leader that day, led us in to a climbing head-on attack.

'I selected one "Zeke" at the right of the formation and started firing. He started smoking and rolled down and to his right. I followed, firing intermittently, to 18,000 ft, then pulled back to rejoin our formation. I had lost my second element and my wingman (Lt Hunt) by this time. My wingman could only drop one belly tank, and because of this could not pull out of his dive until at 4000 ft. He saw the "Zeke" that I had fired on go straight down, still smoking.

'I pulled up behind "Red Flight" at 21,000 ft, and arrived in time to see two Zeros attacking from a position of "four o'clock high". After I had fired at them in an attempt to drive them away, four others started down on me from "six o'clock high", forcing me to dive to 14,000 ft. I had begun a climb when I sighted two "Zekes" at "two o'clock" and 1000 ft below me. I dived in to an attack, getting several shots with no results observed.

'I was at 18,000 ft when three Zekes from "eight o'clock high" attacked me. As I was diving out, one got very close to me and put two "slugs" into the cockpit and possibly other parts of the ship. My evasive manoeuvre in this instance was to increase my dive to vertical, diving to 7000 ft, then pulling up to 13,000 ft.

'At that time I saw seven Zeros in a loose formation and to the rear of a P-38, which appeared to be in trouble. As one Zeke began his pass at the P-38, I made my attack on him from a 90-degree angle of deflection. I fired a long burst and saw him break away in flames. Feeling that I could distract the enemy from the P-38 by making an attack, I pulled up slightly and to the right, getting a direct tail shot. I closed to about 100 ft and began firing. The "Zeke" began burning and rolled slowly to the left and down.

'The remaining "Zekes" attacked me at that time. One was about 100 ft behind me, and closing. As I started to dive out, my left engine began to burn, my right engine was smoking, a cannon shell burst in the radio compartment and a 7.7 mm machine gun shell hit my wrist and embedded itself into the instrument panel. Other shells hit at the base of the control column. I received shrapnel in my right arm and my hips.

'I tried to pull out of the dive but my elevator controls were completely useless. I then released my escape hatch and bailed out. I landed in the sea about 25 miles from shore and remained there for approximately 30 minutes. I was unable to inflate my life raft as it had been holed by shrapnel. I was picked up by Navy PT boat No 152 and carried to PT Tender USS *Hilo* in Buna Bay. (*Cover artwork by Mark Postlethwaite*)

First published in Great Britain in 2007 by Osprey Publishing
Midland House, West Way, Botley, Oxford, OX2 0PH
443 Park Avenue South, New York, NY, 10016, USA
E-mail: info@ospreypublishing.com

© 2007 Osprey Publishing Limited

ISBN 978 1 84603 043 7

Edited by Tony Holmes
Page design by Mark Holt
Cover Artwork by Mark Postlethwaite
Aircraft Profiles by Chris Davey
Index by Alan Thatcher
Originated by PDQ Digital Media Solutions
Printed and bound in China through Bookbuilders

07 08 09 10 11   10 9 8 7 6 5 4 3 2 1

For a catalogue of all books published by Osprey please contact:
NORTH AMERICA
Osprey Direct, C/o Random House Distribution Center,
400 Hahn Road, Westminster, MD 21157
E-mail:info@ospreydirect.com

ALL OTHER REGIONS
Osprey Direct UK, P.O. Box 140 Wellingborough, Northants, NN8 2FA, UK
E-mail: info@ospreydirect.co.uk
www.ospreypublishing.com

ACKNOWLEDGEMENTS
People who helped with photographs or significant bits of data include Michael Bates, David Hoxie, David Mason, Ken Peters and Sandra Delashaw Warden

CONTENTS

INTRODUCTION

There were two clearly crack P-38 Lightning fighter groups in World War 2, namely the 82nd FG in the Mediterranean and the 475th FG in the Southwest Pacific. Both were credited with more than 500 confirmed aerial victories apiece in a remarkably short period of time, and both were staffed with an impressive cadre of highly trained and motivated pilots who transcended the difficulties inherent in their particular operational conditions to create outstanding combat records by war's end.

In the case of the 475th FG, the key to making it an elite combat unit was the personality of Maj Gen George Churchill Kenney, Commander-in-Chief of the USAAF's Fifth Air Force. His dynamic personality and vision for conducting the air war in the Southwest Pacific were responsible for creating a unit that was despised and feared by the Japanese and despised and envied by other USAAF units within V Fighter Command.

The hatred towards the group in Allied ranks came about because Maj Gen Kenney insisted on taking the best personnel from other units, which were in the throes of austere staffing themselves, and creating a cadre of instant fighting elite aviators and groundcrews. Just as Maj Gen Claire Chennault had hastily gathered a group of professional and experienced pilots to become the famed 'Flying Tigers' of the American Volunteer Group in China, Kenney brought together a tough body of men who guaranteed that a whirlwind would be hurled against the enemy once they entered combat.

The list of distinguished accomplishments garnered by the 475th FG is impressive, with perhaps the speed at which its pilots scored aerial victories being the most notable of them all. Averaging about 20 victories a month during the 23 months that it was on operations, the 475th was the fastest scoring fighter group in the Pacific, and among the top ten in the USAAF by war's end. Both of America's leading aces scored at least some of their victories with the group, and, indeed, the two most successful pilots in the Southwest Pacific claimed all of their kills with the 475th.

Throughout its brief combat history the 475th was feared by the enemy, and envied by fellow fighter units for its pick of crews and new equipment in the Fifth Air Force. Many of the best fighter leaders were transferred in to the group from hard-pressed squadrons, in addition to the allocation of the precious few factory-fresh P-38s that made it to the Southwest Pacific. Other units in turn had to be satisfied with combat-weary Lightnings, or other fighter types that were thoroughly obsolescent by 1944. Rivalries with other P-38 groups ensued, but in the end the record of the 475th justified every sacrifice made on its behalf by V Fighter Command.

John Stanaway
Zanesville, Ohio
October 2006

BE JOYFUL IN BATTLE

If circumstances had taken their normal course, the 475th FG would have been activated in the middle of 1943, equipped with the P-40N Warhawk and left to become an ordinary line unit without being given the chance to write the distinguished military history that it eventually did. As it happened, the combination of a firebrand commanding general (Maj Gen George C Kenney) conferring with an equally resourceful US Army Head-of-General Staff (Gen George C Marshall), along with an unusually talented group of combat pilots and crews, would severely challenge the enemy and write a remarkable page of history in the Southwest Pacific air war.

The 475th was activated by special authority granted to the Fifth Air Force on 14 May 1943, one day before the group was constituted within the auspices of the United States Army Air Forces (USAAF). Maj Gen Kenney had his work cut out when it came to staffing his new fighter unit since he had to find the pilots and groundcrews from within V Fighter Command. In addition to seeking out good people for the unit, he had to locate pilots who could fly ultra-long range escort missions, which would be the norm from then on in the Southwest Pacific. Few aviators had the training or experience to conduct such 300+ mile flights, whilst still defending the bombers against very potent Japanese defences.

There were three essential sources for the first cadre of 475th aircrew. The core of the new unit would come from the already painfully understaffed groups of V Fighter Command. Five or six pilots would have to be sliced from the lean flesh of each of the nine hard-pressed operational squadrons within the command at the time, and Kenney had specified that none of the choices could be sub-par material. The first groans of displeasure were soon heard from harried squadron commanders who were required to part with men that they felt were the lifeblood of their units.

Another avenue explored by Kenney was the relatively dormant Seventh Air Force based in Hawaii. Following its action during the Pearl Harbor attack on 7 December 1941, the 15th FG had been less than fully utilised from an operational standpoint. Kenney had already benefitted from the Seventh Air Force in the late summer of 1942, when he brought in future aces 1Lt Harry Brown, who had claimed a 'Val' dive-bomber during the Pearl Harbor attack and scored further kills with the 49th and 475th FGs, and 1Lt Verl Jett, who initially joined the 8th FG and would eventually command the 475th FG's 431st FS.

A number of pilots transferred directly from the 15th FG to the 475th in July 1943, including 1Lts John Cohn, John Knox and Paul Morriss, who went into the 431st, 1Lts Billy Gresham and Howard Hedrick, who joined the 432nd, and 1Lts Ralph Cleague and Robert Tomberg who were assigned to the 433rd. These pilots were not given any details about their new assignment, but the tacit promise of action appealed to them more than the scant opportunities to fight the enemy in the quiet sector of the middle Pacific.

Ex-15th FG pilot 1Lt Howard Hedrick was amongst the first recruits for the 431st FS, and he is seen here at Amberly Field soon after the arrival of his P-38H-1 (*Krane*)

Lt Col George W Prentice was the first CO of the newly-formed 475th FG, having been posted in from the 8th FG's 39th FS. Although a fearless fighter pilot, Prentice was not a natural when it came to engaging the enemy, so he left leadership of group combat formations to his more capable squadron COs. Prentice's organisational skills on the ground were second to none, however, and he proved a boon to the group once it arrived in New Guinea in August 1943 (*Cooper*)

Others transferring into the Fifth Air Force were 1Lt Martin Low, who would briefly serve with the 40th FS/35th FG before taking command of the 433rd FS/475th FG, and 1Lt Joe McKeon, who scored a victory in the P-39-equipped 35th FS/8th FG, before becoming an ace with the 433rd.

Despite bringing in these pilots from the combat 'backwaters', V Fighter Command primarily relied on the sacrifices made by existing squadrons in-theatre when it came to staffing the 475th FG. The 8th FG's 39th FS contributed six pilots, in addition to veteran groundcrews and its own commander, Lt Col George Prentice, who was made CO of the 475th on 21 May 1943. The 431st FS was a direct beneficiary of this infusion of talent from the 49th FG, with its first commanding officer being Maj Franklin A Nichols, late of the 7th FS. 1Lts David Allen, Harry Brown, Jack Mankin and Arthur Wenige, who all joined from the 49th at this time, duly made their mark by achieving ace status with the 475th.

Frank Nichols already had four aerial victories to his name following his service with the 7th FS's piquantly named flight, 'Nick Nichols' Nip Nippers'. Nichols was perfectly suited to the spirit of the new 475th FG, and his exuberance and tenacity eventually saw him become a full general in the postwar USAF. His dynamic personality and whirlwind nature served the 431st FS well during its first days in action, and many of the remarkable records set by the 475th in its first actions were largely made possible because of Nichols' energy at the head of his squadron. Indeed, he was only slightly fatigued when he handed the reins of the unit over to Maj Verl Jett in November 1943.

Equally talented personnel came to the 432nd FS between May and July 1943, with Maj Frank Tompkins, Capt James Ince and 1Lt Noel Lundy being transferred in from the 80th FS/8th FG. Tompkins was the 432nd's first CO, and Ince served as interim commander for a time too. Future 432nd FS CO 1Lt John Loisel joined from the 36th FS/8th FG at this time too, and he would subsequently rise through the ranks to become the 475th FG's final wartime commander.

Loisel was a tall and lean officer with a taciturn, but genial, manner. He was, in fact, a signal leader in the orientation and training of pilots into service with the P-38. With brisk aplomb, Loisel was largely responsible for assuring that pilots assigned to the new group were indoctrinated in the efficient operation of the Lockheed fighter, as well as the unusual air discipline needed for aerial combat tactics. His stewardship ensured, for example, that pilots knew how to use the emergency features of the P-38, like single-engine operation and the manual employment of hydraulically-operated functions, as well as the importance of maintaining flight integrity and radio discipline in the combat area.

Naturally, the formation of a new offensive fighter force was heavily wrapped in secrecy, so those selected for the unit were unaware of the specific reason for their transfer. It was theatre policy to weed out pilots who had been involved in more than one aircraft crash, or who had shown undisciplined behaviour in operational conditions. Some of the men selected for the 475th were therefore convinced that they had made some indiscretion which marked them for banishment. Only when large groups of highly qualified pilots and other personnel were gathered at air depots for transportation to Australia did the exciting rumour spread that exceptional crews were being assembled for a special assignment.

One of the mechanics involved was Sgt Carl A King, formerly of the 9th FS, where he had worked on both P-38 and P-40 engines, before he and the others selected from his unit were packed off to Australia on 29 June 1943;

'We took off from Port Moresby and landed at Seven-Mile aerodrome at about 0815 hrs, and then went to Ward's aerodrome to get an aeroplane to Townsville, in Queensland. By 1128 hrs we were in the air once again in a C-47 headed out to sea – at Ward's, we saw four of the new four-engined Douglas C-54 transports. We landed at Garbutt Field, in Townsville, at 1600 hrs, ate and then got a train south at 2200 hrs that same night. We stayed on the train for two days and two nights, and at 0630 hrs on Thursday, 1 July 1943, we pulled into Brisbane. There were trucks there to take us to Amberly Field, and by 0730 hrs we were at our new home, which was cold as hell.'

Sgt King would soon find himself working on one of the 75 brand new P-38Hs assigned to the 475th, which would arrive at Amberly Field in gradual increments over coming weeks.

If the remaining squadrons of the Fifth Air Force had reason to resent the preferential treatment given to the new group, then there would have been justification for open revolt from other USAAF commands had they got wind of the deployment of scarce P-38s to the Pacific. Three groups in the Mediterranean, with two more scheduled to relieve the long range bomber escort shortage in England, had to be content with what they could scrounge from the meagre stocks of available P-38s. The formation and equipping of the 475th had to be kept secret from the USAAF's overseas commands, as well as the enemy!

At unit level, Sgt King was assigned to 'B Flight' in the 431st FS, and he saw his charge for the first time on 8 July 1943. He and his fellow groundcrew immediately began working on the P-38, which gave them 'holy trouble' until the 432nd FS borrowed it and reported no trouble.

The latter squadron received its first Lightning – a combat-weary P-38G-5 presumably from a service unit that repaired worn and damaged aircraft and assigned them to different units – which was charged to the care of the squadron's engineering section on 23 June. By the end of that month the 432nd had taken delivery of an additional six P-38Hs.

Maj Al Schinz, who had seen combat in P-39s and P-400s in New Guinea with the 41st FS/35th FG in 1942-43, became the 475th FG's first executive officer (*Cooper***)**

The squadron's personnel strength was also increased with the addition of Capt Danny Roberts as operations officer, Capt Arsenio Fernandez as adjutant and Capt Ronald Malloch as intelligence officer. Roberts had already enjoyed success with the 80th FS, scoring two kills with the P-39 and two with the P-38 before his old unit reluctantly gave him up to the 475th FG. Roberts would go on to attain legendary status with the 432nd FS, claiming three more victories before joining the 433rd FS as its CO in October 1943. He downed a further seven Japanese fighters with his new unit prior to being killed in a mid-air collision with another P-38H shortly after securing his 14th victory on 9 November 1943.

Things were not quite as felicitous in the formation of the 433rd, however. A perfectly sound line pilot who had little in the way of administrative experience was selected to command the new squadron, newly-promoted Capt Martin Low, formerly of the 40th FS/35th FG, making some immediately unpopular decisions, not the least of which was an unfortunate choice for First Sergeant. The new top enlisted man in the squadron showed an immediate disdain for subordinates, and his treatment of the enlisted grades made him greatly disliked, subsequently causing morale on the line to drop precipitously.

The disfavour extended, justly or unjustly, to the squadron commander himself, who had a reputation as a fairly good combat formation leader, but was forced to take increasingly tougher measures on the ground in order to retain some semblance of control of his unit. One of Low's most hated orders was the removal of names from the promotion lists unless the individual concerned was shown to be well-deserving.

Veteran pilots from the 433rd generally saw Capt Low in a more kindly light, and the latter eventually went home on rotation in early October 1943 and subsequently saw further combat as CO of the Eighth Air Force's P-38-equipped 55th FS/20th FG in 1944, during which time he

This overhead view of Amberly Field was taken in early July 1943, and it shows the 475th FG's camp in the background and all six of the group's P-38Hs in the foreground. A further 69 Lightnings had arrived at the base by month-end (*Cooper*)

won a Silver Star. The First Sergeant has remained nameless over the decades, enlisted 433rd veterans being reluctant to mention him.

The squadron's early combat results suffered because of the generally low spirit of the 433rd, but things would dramatically improve once Capt Danny Roberts took charge on 3 October 1943.

TRAINING AND FIRST COMBAT

Although events at Amberly slowly began to evolve into some sort of military order as July 1943 progressed, Col Prentice drew concern from his veteran pilots for his apparently clueless approach to aerial combat. He was reputed to be a fearless fighter pilot, but some of his wingmen claim that they were often left to frantically deal with enemy aircraft that he had allowed to get onto his tail.

Fortunately, Prentice apparently saw the light (or was shown it!) and left leadership of group combat formations to more capable pilots, instead preferring to focus his attention on his penchant for ground organisation. One of the important points that Prentice tried to emphasise early on was group coherence and integrity of formations in the air. However, when the author mentioned this focus on group integrity to random veterans from the 475th, he was greeted with baffled shrugs. There was fierce loyalty within the squadrons, but apparently no desire to identify closely with the other units.

Having said that, the matter of formation discipline was stressed to the point of reflex action from the minute the group was established. There were a few mavericks who ventured off on their own at times, but in general the 475th was distinctive in its adherence to maintaining at least flights of four. As a result, the Japanese came to recognise the red, yellow or blue spinners of large flights of P-38s diving down on their formations, and referred to this dangerous enemy in unkind terms – even before they had an inkling of the 475th's real identity.

Training began as soon as P-38s were available for service. Sgt King mentioned in his journal that he had many difficulties with the first Lightnings given over to his charge. Frequently, he would work throughout the night to bring his aircraft to flying status, only to have supply shortages force him into inactivity for days when he could not get the right parts to fix his fighter. Sgt King's experience was common for the servicing crews of the neophyte group, but the intervals of inactivity were not inordinately suffered since the pleasures of Brisbane were easily available, and popular with crews used to the privations of jungle camps.

Of course there were unfortunate results to the initial disorder of the organisation. One of the first caused the death of 431st FS pilot 1Lt Richard Dotson, whose P-38 crashed and burned during an attempted landing on 5 July 1943. Records indicate that four days later fellow squadron pilot 1Lt Andrew K Duke was killed when he crashed flying 431st FS P-38 '136' at Mareeba, in northern Australia. Capt Harry Brown damaged number '118' by running into a tree, and number '122' had a taxiing accident at around the same time.

One positive feature of the organisation of the group in Australia was the presence of resourceful requisitions people. The first 475th camp was established at Amberly in June 1943, with the appearance of neat rows of tents and several buildings of wood, canvas, concrete and screening to fend off the various insects that dominated the area. Talented supply officer Capt Claude Stubbs, aided by 1Lt Davis and Sgts Bryant and Joseph, developed reputations for gathering materials necessary for the group to attain operational status. By the end of July the 475th was beginning to look like a frontline organisation on the ground, although its formations still left a lot to be desired in the air.

Technical inspection of group engineering was initially entrusted to World War 1 veteran Capt Albert Dossett. He had served in the Army for 26 years by the time he finally rotated home, and was reputed to have taken no leave while assigned to the 475th. His place was taken by Capt Bill Pruss, who had been doing the job for the 432nd FS. Pruss, in turn, was replaced by CWO Greg Kowalski in the 432nd FS, and the latter was eventually succeeded by redoubtable nine-kill ace 1Lt Joe Forster when Kowalski also returned home on rotation.

Training of pilots and groundcrews progressed in Queensland until late July 1943, when the pressing state of the Pacific war dictated that the group be thrown into action now that they had achieved an acceptable standard of operational proficiency. By the end of the month the 475th had begun its ponderous movement northwards, sending air and ground echelons to Port Moresby, on the southern coast of New Guinea. Sgt King watched his P-38 leave Amberly on 29 July, and he was now anxious to get back into action following his brief time in Queensland. In the interim, King received another brand-new Lightning;

'I got a new ship today and she is a "beaut" – P-38H-5-LO 42-66742, complete with a new paint job. I also loaded ten $2^{1}/_{2}$-ton trucks today with equipment to be sent by boat on our trip north.'

King's new Lightning would see action in the very first engagement fought by the group, the aircraft clashing with Japanese fighters on the afternoon of 16 August 1943 when future five-kill ace, and ex-9th FS/49th FG pilot, 1Lt Jack Mankin was credited with the destruction of a 'Zeke' and a Ki-43 'Oscar' over Marilinan. Two days later Capt Verl Jett

This informal portrait of mostly 431st FS aircrew was taken at Port Moresby soon after the unit arrived in New Guinea in August 1943. Standing, from left to right, are O'Brien, Knox, Morris, Samms, Champlin, Elliott, McBreen, Cline, Czarnecki, Bellows, Dunlap, Kirby and Brown. Kneeling, again from left to right, are Smith, Allen, Wenige, Phillips, Hood, Blythe, Jett, Hedrick, Lewis, Gronemeyer, Houseworth, Lent, Cohn. Thirteen of these pilots would become aces with the 475th and three would be killed in action (*Cooper*)

used 42-66742 to destroy a pair of 'Zekes' over Wewak.

Perhaps because the personnel involved with the group were a cut above the ordinary combat crews in-theatre due to their previous front-line experience, the final stages of the 475th's training and organisation rapidly took shape once it reached New Guinea in early August. Tension built in anticipation of the first operational mission, and 431st FS records suggest that the unit's provision of escorts for transports heading to Tsili Tsili on 12 August marked the group's combat debut. However, the lack of any documen-

Dubbed the 'Terrible Four' of the 431st FS for their exploits both on the ground and in the air, Harry Brown, John Hood, Frank Nichols and William Haning provided the squadron with its fighting spirit during its first months in combat from Port Moresby (*Cooper*)

tation surrounding this operation suggests that it was either cancelled or assigned to another group.

The 432nd FS had followed the 431st FS to Port Moresby by the 12th, and the unit flew its first mission the very next day when Capt Danny Roberts led 15 P-38s on a three-hour escort of transports again bound for Tsili Tsili. Although this proved to be little more than a routine flight, seven future aces (Roberts, James 'Impossible' Ince, Fred 'Square Loop' Harris, John Loisel, Paul Lucas, Billy Gresham and Grover Gholson) got some valuable operational flight time in the P-38 under their belts.

Theatre-wide, aerial opposition was certainly heating up as aggressive American combat formations sought to engage Japanese fighters and bombers over their home bases. For example, just 24 hours after the 432nd FS had completed its escort mission to Tsili Tsili, P-39s from the 35th FG downed more than ten Japanese aircraft in exactly the same area. On the 16th it would be the 431st FS's turn to take on the enemy – and thus provide the 475th FG with its first victories – during yet another transport escort mission, this time to Marilinan.

Squadron Mission No 5 began at 1225 hrs when 15 P-38s took off to rendezvous with their charges. The first sight of the enemy came at about 1520 hrs over Marilinan, when the 431st's pilots, who were cruising at 21,000 ft, looked up just in time to spot 15+ Japanese fighters diving down on them from the northeast. The P-38 pilots immediately dived away and took violent evasive action in an effort to avoid a disaster at the hands of the enemy in their very first encounter.

Capt Harry Brown (in P-38H-1 42-66592) was listening to warnings from his fighter controller when he heard 1Lt David Allen (in P-38H-5 42-66744) shout over the radio that he was being attacked from the rear. Brown then saw eight enemy fighters descending towards him too, so he pushed the nose of his P-38 down and led his flight out of harm's way. Once he thought that it was safe to turn into the sun so as to regain the initiative, he wheeled the Lightnings back in the direction of Marilinan.

Brown was able to see 1Lt Allen shoot the wing off an 'Oscar' and send another aircraft, tentatively identified as a B5N 'Kate' torpedo-bomber, down in flames. When other Japanese fighters began closing in on the

13

Capt Harry Brown became the first pilot within the 475th FG to attain ace status when he claimed three Ki-43s destroyed whilst flying this P-38H-1 (42-66592) over Marilinan during the group's first encounter with the enemy on 16 August 1943. These victories were added to a single 'Val' dive-bomber that he had downed whilst flying a P-36A with the 47th PS/15th PG during the Pearl Harbor attack on 7 December 1941 and a Ki-43 that he had destroyed flying a P-38G-15 with the 9th FS/49th FG in New Guinea on 4 March 1943. Brown would subsequently claim a 'Zeke' on 24 October 1943 for his sixth, and final, victory (*Cooper*)

remaining flights, Brown led his own P-38s down into the fight and chased away at least one enemy aircraft with an inconclusive burst of fire.

Climbing once again to regain the advantage of altitude, Brown sighted another 'Oscar' (he identified it as a 'Zeke') above him and carefully aimed from dead astern until his fire caused an explosion in the fighter's cockpit. He then lined up a second Ki-43 in his gunsight and shared in its destruction with another P-38. Finally, a third 'Oscar' pulled up into a hammerhead stall directly in front of Brown's fighter, which hit the Japanese fighter so hard with cannon and machine gun shells that the Ki-43 exploded while it was almost motionless at the top of the stall.

1Lt Lowell Lutton (in P-38H-1 42-66548) was leading the last Lightning flight into the heart of the fight when he and his wingman, 2Lt Orville Blythe, were separated from the second element. They charged head-on at two 'Oscars', and the first Japanese fighter turned away while Lutton shot off part of the engine and canopy of the second – Blythe saw the Ki-43 spin away into the jungle below. The latter's P-38 had been so badly damaged in the head-on pass that he had to make a forced landing at Marilinan's airstrip. Prior to setting his fighter down, Blythe had also witnessed the crash of the second 'Oscar' credited to 1Lt Art Wenige (in P-38H-1 42-66511) during the course of the mission.

As previously mentioned, 1Lt Jack Mankin had taken Sgt King's P-38 into the fray and shot down an 'Oscar' that burst into flames after the Lightning pilot had opened fire from close range. Then Mankin and his wingman, 2Lt Paul Smith, attacked another Ki-43 and an aircraft that looked like a 'Kate' dive-bomber. Mankin destroyed the 'Oscar' and Smith set the B5N alight. Mankin was impressed with Smith, who had managed to stay with him throughout the entire engagement.

Good fortune allowed the 431st FS to claim 12 victories following this clash, with only 1Lt Blythe's P-38 being damaged in return. It had been a

morale-building engagement which had reinforced the training and tactics drummed into the 475th's pilots by the group's senior officers.

Among the future aces claiming their first kills on this day was 1Lt Warren Lewis (in P-38H-5 42-66737), who would subsequently destroy a further six aircraft and lead the 433rd FS from November 1943 through to August 1944. His combat report for 16 August 1943 detailed the action as follows;

'At 1525 hrs I saw two flights of Zeros attack "Red Flight" over the strip, so I dropped tanks and led "White Flight" on a rear quarter pass. Zeros broke off climbing. I then turned to the north and saw a flight of Zeros attacking a P-47 flight. I made a 60-degree deflection pass on a Zero chasing a P-47, firing from 150 to 350 yards. The Zero, which was of the "Oscar" type, went into a roll as if hit. I passed over him, and after turning, I could not find him. I do not make any claim for the destruction of enemy aircraft.'

Nonetheless, Lewis was given credit for a kill after Allied personnel at Tsili Tsili had seen the Ki-43 crash following his attack. Confirmation reached the group through eyewitness testimony that was transmitted via the 40th FS/35th FG. This victory only added to the 475th's jubilation, and the group went on to claim even greater successes in coming days.

WEWAK CAMPAIGN

475th FG formations mounted the group's first bomber escort to the Japanese fortress at Wewak on 17 August, although they took the enemy by such surprise that very few enemy fighters managed to get into the air to oppose the strike. The P-38s covered B-25s that were sent in at low-level to drop parachute bombs on the parked enemy aircraft at the main airfield in the area. Some 50 Japanese fighters and bombers were destroyed, although only a handful of these were actually shot down.

Pilots relax between scrambles in the 475th FG Alert Shack at Port Moresby in the late summer of 1943. The individuals visible in this photograph are, middle row, from left to right, Veit, Monk, Lent, Allen and unknown. In the background are Kirby and Morris, and in the foreground are Samms and Houseworth (*Cooper*)

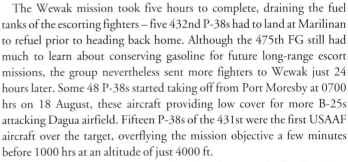

The Wewak mission took five hours to complete, draining the fuel tanks of the escorting fighters – five 432nd P-38s had to land at Marilinan to refuel prior to heading back home. Although the 475th FG still had much to learn about conserving gasoline for future long-range escort missions, the group nevertheless sent more fighters to Wewak just 24 hours later. Some 48 P-38s started taking off from Port Moresby at 0700 hrs on 18 August, these aircraft providing low cover for more B-25s attacking Dagua airfield. Fifteen P-38s of the 431st were the first USAAF aircraft over the target, overflying the mission objective a few minutes before 1000 hrs at an altitude of just 4000 ft.

Once again, the Japanese seemed to have been caught flat-footed, as only a handful of 'Oscars' from the 24th Sentai were encountered on patrol. These aircraft reported spotting a force of 40 American aircraft heading north over Hansa Bay, which in turn resulted in the immediate scrambling of seven more 'Oscars' from the 24th Sentai, five Ki-61 'Tony' fighters from the 68th Sentai and two twin-engined Ki-45 'Nicks' from 13th Sentai – all these aircraft were based at Borum. Nine Ki-43s from the 59th Sentai at But airfield also intercepted the raid.

The 431st FS pilots soon sighted enemy fighters above them as they raced over Dagua airfield in an effort to sweep it clean of any aerial opposition for the approaching B-25s. They all switched to internal fuel before dropping their external tanks in preparation for the impending fight. The weather had been reasonably clear en route to Wewak, but now it was clouding over. Sporadic showers were encountered as the P-38 pilots watched the Japanese fighters dive down on them.

1Lt Don Bellows of the 431st FS poses for the camera alongside an early P-38F that featured a side-hinging canopy. Bellows would score an early victory for the group when he claimed an 'Oscar' on the 18 August 1943 bomber escort mission to Wewak (*Cooper*)

1Lt Lowell Lutton (in P-38H-1 42-66548) was an old hand from the 8th FS/49th FG, and he was leading 'Blue Flight' when he followed 'Red' and 'White' flights up into the enemy attack. The B-25s had just hit their target, and the 431st was inland of the Japanese airstrip, so Lutton felt confident that he could concentrate on the enemy fighters while the bombers retreated over the sea.

An 'Oscar' pulled up in front of Lutton's P-38, allowing him to fire inconclusively before having to break off his attack. He then saw another Ki-43 falling in flames, and Lutton later learned that flightmate 1Lt Don Bellows had shot it down.

Lutton had lost his flight in the subsequent wild manoeuvring over Wewak, so he quickly found two other P-38s that were soon the focus of attention for a determined 'Oscar' pilot who made a head-on attack. When the two Lightnings broke after passing the enemy fighter, Lutton

431st FS pilots eagerly listen to Capt Haning as he briefs an early transport escort mission in his capacity as group operations officer in mid August 1943. An Australian Army liaison officer can be seen observing Capt Haning's brief – perhaps the transports were conducting a supply drop in support of Australian troops in the field? (*Cooper*)

succeeded in getting in a good shot at the Ki-43, which burst into flames and fell away into the jungle below.

Now alone once again, Lutton quickly joined up with two more P-38s which, coincidentally, endured yet another head-on pass from a solitary 'Oscar'. This time, however, all three Lightning pilots got on the tail of the wildly gyrating enemy fighter, but only Lutton managed to follow him long enough to get in some good shots when the Ki-43 turned away from Dagua airstrip and headed out to sea. The P-38 pilot overshot the 'Oscar', and when Lutton looked back he could not find his foe. He did, however, see flames on the surface of the water from what must have been a crashed enemy aircraft. Lutton then joined up with other P-38s to cover the retreating B-25s.

The first two Lightnings that Lutton had tried to formate with early on in the engagement had been flown by 1Lts Tom McGuire (in P-38H-1 42-66592) and 2Lt 'Fran' Lent (in P-38H-1 42-66550). Lutton had seen at least one 'Oscar' shot down by the pair, and it is a matter of record that McGuire was credited with the destruction of two Ki-43s and a Ki-61 and Lent a 'Hamp' for their first victories.

One indication of the confusion inherent in aerial combat comes from the combat reports lodged by Japanese fighter pilots that survived the 18 August action. 475th records indicate that enemy pilots were skilled and aggressive in this engagement, and Chutai (flight) leader Nanba Shigeki of the 59th Sentai was certainly that. He was leading six 'Oscars' into the battle when he was cut off from his charges by a large number of P-38s. This was his first real encounter with the Lockheed fighter, and he wrote in his report that he was dismayed to find that he could not outrun or out climb it.

Although Shigeki's Ki-43 was hit several times, he was skilled enough to evade destruction by using the breathtaking manoeuvrability of his fighter. When his attackers turned away, apparently satisfied that he was shot down, Shigeki chose to engage his pursuers rather than escape. It can be assumed from some of the 431st after action reports, therefore, that the P-38 pilots were convinced that they were being bounced by an entirely different fighter, rather than the one they had just shot up.

Shigeki was finally able to crash-land his 'Oscar' on But West airfield after the raid subsided. Again, following a careful study of 475th FG after action reports, it is possible that as many as four pilots claimed to have shot the resourceful Shigeki down!

The 432nd FS was also heavily engaged over Wewak on the 18th, and the unit scored its first victory when Capt William Waldman claimed an 'Oscar'. 2Lt Paul Lucas did not manage a kill on this mission, although he filed an after action report that reflected the fury of the clash;

'I was flying the wing of 1Lt Grover Gholson and had just come within sight of But airfield when I heard someone report "Zeros at 'ten o'clock'" and everybody began dropping belly tanks. I dropped mine and made a wide half circle to the left and came back over But on the land side. A Zero was diving away from another P-38, and 1Lt Gholson made a high, tight turn and came in on the Zero's tail. I cut inside and down and got a short full deflection shot at the Zero. I don't think he was hit. The Zero was a bright natural aluminium colour, and had evenly rounded wingtips and a radial engine.

'In pulling out of my dive, I lost 1Lt Gholson and had lost too much altitude, so I went wide and started to climb back up. While climbing, I saw a P-38 chase a Zero in a vertical climb up into a cloud – the Zero did a tight Immelman turn and nosed down into a head-on attack on the P-38. The P-38 broke off and dove away. There didn't seem to be any Zeros left, so I joined seven P-38s headed for Marilinan. I landed there.'

With the destruction of an additional 15 Japanese aircraft by its pilots following this mission, the 475th had achieved an impressive 27 kills in its first two encounters with the enemy. The effort expended by Maj Gen Kenney in creating an elite offensive unit was paying immediate dividends. The group had suffered its first loss on 18 August, however, when 2Lt Ralph Schmidt of the 431st FS failed to return to Port Moresby – he was last seen flying alone after becoming separated from his flight.

Yet another sparkling performance was put in by V Fighter Command's P-38 force during the third strike on Wewak, flown on 21 August. The 475th sortied 33 P-38s for a high cover mission over a force of B-25 Mitchells that left their base at 0730 hrs and arrived overhead the target at 1000 hrs.

1Lt Tom McGuire (again in 42-66592) was leading 'Blue Flight', with 2Lt 'Fran' Lent (in 42-66550) once again flying as his wingman, when calls came in from the low cover fighters requesting help in fending off Japanese interceptors at 3000 ft. McGuire finally sighted the milling dogfight below, and he took his flight down to attack. One 'Oscar' (claimed as a 'Zeke') fell to a 45-degree blast from McGuire's guns, and Lent watched the fighter crash in flames into the jungle below.

Although the second element of McGuire's flight had become separated during this initial contact with the enemy, 1Lt David Allen (in 42-66744) made short work of another 'Oscar' that appeared ahead of him. Both this aircraft and a second Ki-43 that fell to McGuire's fire – giving him ace status – were seen to crash by Allen (who also 'made ace' later that day with three fighters destroyed to add to his previous four kills) and Lent.

McGuire then confirmed the destruction of a twin-engined fighter (possibly a Ki-45) for Lent, which he saw crash into the jungle below. McGuire also claimed to have damaged a twin-engined aircraft after he observed hits on its wing, engine and cockpit. There was in fact only one 'Nick' of the 13th Sentai listed as lost in Japanese records, although no fewer than four American pilots claimed to have destroyed one apiece.

It seems from the language used in the after action reports from the 21st that most of the attackers were firing at the same target, and simply claiming that their fire was doing the job of destruction! In spite of the subsequent controversy that surrounded the legendary Tom McGuire, it may at least be said of him that he was prudent in making his claims on this particular occasion.

Capt Danny Roberts (in P-38H-1 42-66513) also had a fruitful day whilst leading the 432nd FS's 'Clover' (unit call-sign) flights. Ordering his 14 Lightnings down to protect the B-25s, which were under attack by 'Oscars' and 'Tonys', his flight became embroiled in a swirling dogfight when still more Japanese fighters bounced the P-38s. The 432nd FS pilots claimed 12 enemy aircraft shot down, two of them confirmed for Roberts (he stated that they were 'Hamps' rather than Ki-43s), which gave him ace status – he already had four kills to his name from his P-400/P-38 days with the 80th FS/8th FG.

1Lts Fred 'Squareloop' Harris (in P-38H-1 42-66553) and John Loisel (in P-38H-1 42-66537) each claimed two 'Tonys', 1Lt Campbell Wilson downed two 'Nicks' and 2Lt Billy Gresham (in P-38H-5 42-66750) and 1Lt Grover Gholson (in P-38H-1 42-66633) a 'Nick' apiece. Finally, 2Lts Elliott Summer (in P-38H-1 42-66575) and Paul Lucas (in P-38H-1 42-66555) each destroyed single 'Oscars', which they identified as 'Zekes' at the time.

1Lt Loisel had been leading the second element of 'White Flight' on the approach to Wewak when he heard Roberts give the order to drop tanks over the radio. He later reported;

'I saw P-38s and enemy fighters at a distance straight ahead of me. We all dropped our tanks when our leader dropped his at 9000 ft. I made successive passes at an inline fighter (a "Tony"), two Zeros (probably Ki-43s) and a twin-engined fighter. Then I saw a yellow-nosed Zero, high at "seven o'clock", close and shooting. I dived with my wingman across in front of another element and lost him. I then made a head-on pass at a twin-engined fighter and fired at a Zero in a slight bank at "two o'clock". He passed close under my left wing. My wingman, 2Lt Lucas, also fired and hit him – he saw him burn.

'I made my next pass at an inline fighter and followed up with a head-on pass at close quarters. I saw the wing of my foe peeling off in large

A veteran of 83 combat missions over New Guinea in P-39s and P-400s with the 36th FS/8th FG in 1942-43, 1Lt John Loisel brought much needed combat experience to the 475th FG. He proved his worth to the group early on when he scored his first two victories – both Ki-61s – over Wewak on 21 August 1943 (*Author*)

19

Future ten-kill ace 2Lt Elliott Summer of the 432nd FS strikes a pose in a rarely seen flying jacket during his time with the group in Queensland in July 1943. Such thick apparel was only appropriate for winter flying in Australia, and had no place in the hot and humid weather of the Southwest Pacific (*Author*)

pieces, and I believe that one of these pieces struck 2Lt Lucas' wing. I claim this aircraft destroyed.

'A single P-38 was then spotted in the general vicinity of Borum, with five or six enemy aircraft dodging in and out of the clouds just over the hills behind it. I dived down on a "Tony" just as it began to roll out on the tip of an Immelman. I pressed home my attack to within 50 yards. The pilot never completed the full roll. Instead, he fell away trailing smoke and out of control. As he was at low altitude (1500 ft), I am sure that he could not have pulled out. The clouds were at my level, and as he fell one passed between us, so I did not see him crash. I claim this aircraft destroyed. Shortly thereafter, I ran out of ammunition and followed my leader away. Initially landing at Tsili Tsili, I returned to base after refuelling.'

Squadronmate 2Lt Elliot Summer recorded a spectacular victory about five minutes after he saw 'Squareloop' Harris destroy his first 'Tony' – aside from the two Ki-61s that he shot down, Harris also damaged four more 'Tonys'. Summer's victim smoked badly for several seconds before bursting into flames and exploding. He then witnessed Harris shoot another Ki-61 off the tail of 432nd FS pilot 2Lt Tom McGuire (not the 431st FS ace). The latter's P-38 was one of the few to suffer any kind of damage during this mission when one of its engines was shot out. Several others were also holed, but all 475th FG aircraft eventually made it home.

As 2Lt Summer left Wewak, he looked back to see at least five Japanese aircraft heading to their bases trailing smoke behind them. At that point he was too occupied with staying with other P-38s and vacating the area to note if any of them subsequently crashed.

21 August had seen the group fly yet another long mission that required a number of pilots to land at Marilinan short of fuel. To a man, they were glad to be down on solid ground after a hard fight.

Sgt King noted the mission, and its cost on his efforts to keep aircraft operational, in the following entry in his journal;

'Got my ship in commission and we pulled the ninth mission today to Wewak. Capt Nichols (in P-38H-1 42-66540) got one and then almost got killed – his ship is shot all to hell, but he is now an ace. 1Lt Allen got three, which made him an ace too. 1Lt McGuire claimed two to become an ace also. 2Lt Lent got two for his first kills, and the squadron now has a total of 35 aircraft shot down in just two weeks of combat time. We only have 19 P-38s left, however. So far we (431st FS) have lost "110", "111", "114", "117", "122" and "123".'

The 431st FS's Capts Frank Nichols and Harry Brown and 1Lts David Allen and Tom McGuire were all now aces with at least five aerial victories to their credit, although only McGuire had claimed all of his kills with the 475th FG. Allen was the leading ace in the group with seven confirmed victories, five of them having been scored with the 431st, while Brown had become the group's first ace on 16 August when his three Ki-43s were combined with two victories he had scored in 1941-42. Nichols' solitary P-38 kill was added to four victories he had claimed while flying P-40Ks with the 7th FS/49th FG in 1942-43 to give him ace status.

The 475th FG had paid a modest price for this success – two pilots killed in training, one lost in an operational accident and another posted missing in action.

The 14th, and final, mission flown to Wewak in August 1943 was mounted on the 29th when 30 P-38s from the 475th FG helped escort B-24s on a high altitude strike. Seven Japanese interceptors were claimed to have been destroyed by the group, three of which fell to the 431st FS. One 'Oscar' was claimed by 1Lt Harold Holze and another Ki-43 and a Ki-61 were downed by 1Lt Tom McGuire (flying his favourite 42-66592) to give him seven confirmed aerial victories. He was now tied with 1Lt David Allen as the group's top scorer.

This mission showed a remarkable aspect of Tom McGuire's emerging nature as a pilot. A veteran of combat in the Aleutians and New Guinea with the 54th PG and 49th FG respectively, his numerous experences in action seemed to have instilled in him an utter fearlessness when it came to engaging the enemy. Some of McGuire's squadron mates became convinced that he was almost eerily talented, while others believed that he was not much more than an ordinary pilot with an enormous amount of drive to become the leading American fighter ace of all time.

The 433rd FS drafted in six pilots from the 39th FS/35th FG, as well as a handful of the unit's P-38s. One of the latter is seen here with sharksmouths on its engine nacelles – a marking applied to virtually all 39th FS Lightnings. This aircraft was brought to the 433rd FS by 1Lt Charles Grice when he joined the 475th FG in July 1943 (*Krane*)

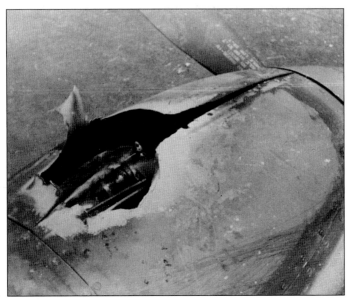

1Lt Tom McGuire's highly successful P-38H-1 42-66592 *PUDGY* was written off charge after it suffered irreparable damage from heavy calibre fire from Japanese fighters on 29 August 1943. With his left engine knocked out, McGuire was forced to make an emergency landing at Marilinan. Prior to his fighter being shot up, the Lightning ace had used *PUDGY* to score his sixth and seventh victories (*Alder*)

McGuire's combat report for the 29 August mission gives some indication of the enigma that he would become;

'I was leading "Blue Flight". We took off from Berry aerodrome (Port Moresby) at 0615 hrs. My wingman "snafued" shortly after take-off so I led a three-ship flight over the target. I saw three medium-sized ships in or near Bogia Harbour.

'At 1050 hrs I saw two Zeros making a pass at the bombers at 17,000-18,000 ft. We dropped belly tanks and I led my flight in – the Zeros ("Oscars") saw us and dived away to the left. I lost my flight at that point. The lead ship pulled up and I got several good bursts at him. The Zero started straight down smoking, then blossomed into flames. This Zero was silver-coloured with a dull finish. I made a pass at another Zero but with no results observed.

'At this time I saw a "Tony" start in at the bombers. I made a head-on pass and then, turning, got several shots in deflection, seeing him lose height whilst smoking and on fire. Being at 13,000 ft, I started back for altitude when I noticed three Zeros and a "Tony" coming down on my tail. Tracers started going by as I stuck my nose down and gave it the throttle. The Zero farthest to the left shot out my left engine, setting it on fire. I shut the engine down and let the propeller windmill, slipping down to 9000 ft and thus putting the fire out – I also used this slipping as an evasive tactic. Two of the enemy fighters followed me down shooting, and I continued on in a 45-degree dive. They left me just before I entered clouds at 4000 ft.'

'I continued on toward the mountains under scattered clouds, then on to Marilinan, where I made a one-engine landing. I left my ship there and returned to base by transport the next day.

'Flak during this mission had been intense, and it appeared to be accurately aimed at the bombers flying between 16,000 ft and 20,000 ft. Enemy tactics were studied and effective. They sent some fighters down at the bombers, but kept others back which eventually dived on us when we attacked those aircraft trying to reach the B-24s. They also had some fighters positioned below the heavy bombers, attacking their vulnerable undersides. The Japanese fighter pilots appeared to be both experienced and eager.'

Tom McGuire's first Lightning (P-38H-1 42-66592, which he nicknamed *PUDGY*) was written off charge at Marilinan following the 29 August mission. Stuck miles from home, McGuire hastily made his report to the 35th FG. 41st FS intelligence officer 1Lt Samuel Yorty made a final general remark to describe the cool nerve of the young 475th fighter ace after debriefing him;

'This pilot remained calm in spite of the fire in his engine, and thereby successfully brought himself and his aeroplane safely to this base.'

HUON GULF AND RABAUL

Both Japanese and Allied records agree that Wewak had endured a series of hard blows that left it reeling by September 1943. Maj Gen George Kenney was satisfied that his air forces could now take the war to the enemy, at least on a limited scale, and he reported this fact to Gen Douglas MacArthur, Supreme Commander of Allied Forces in the Southwest Pacific Area. MacArthur was ultimately determined to make a triumphant return to the Philippines, and the route to his objective had to be over the northern coast of New Guinea in order to both clear the enemy from his flanks and to be within bombing range of the myriad Philippine islands occupied by Japanese forces.

One immediate logistical problem that had plagued the 475th FG throughout the Wewak offensive was eased on the last day of August when the group began its relocation from its various Port Moresby airstrips to Dobodura, on the northern coast of New Guinea. This new base was at least 20 minutes flying time closer to Wewak, and was much more in the sphere of action for the vital areas of New Britain and the Bismarck Sea. The 432nd FS's Capt Danny Roberts led the first air contingent to Dobodura on 31 August.

The legendary Capt Daniel T Roberts only led the 433rd FS for 37 days in October-November 1943, but his confidence both in the air and on the ground transformed his command from being a good squadron into an inspired one (*Cooper*)

By September 1943 the Fifth Air Force was well poised to support an Allied offensive against Japanese bases in eastern New Guinea, as well as those further along the northern coast. Attacks against Wewak continued, nevertheless, and the 433rd FS at last achieved its first aerial kills during one such operation on 2 September, when it was tasked with escorting B-25s sent to bomb the still formidable stronghold. Elsewhere, formations of V Fighter Command P-38s covered B-17s and B-26s attacking Cape Gloucester, on the island of New Britain.

Amongst the pilots conducting the Wewak escort was 2Lt Calvin 'Bud' Wire (in P-38H-1 42-66539), who was wingman to Capt Herbert Jordan in the last 'Possum' (the 433rd's call-sign) flight. Known as a 'little scrapper', Wire had commenced his military flying career with the Royal Canadian Air Force in 1941, prior to transferring to the USAAF in the wake of the Pearl Harbor attack. Whilst performing his duty protecting his leader, Wire would shoot down an 'Oscar' (misidentified as a 'Zeke') for the squadron's first confirmed claim.

As 'Possum' flight neared Wewak, Wire was distressed to find that he had fallen several hundred yards behind his leader. It was then that he spotted Japanese fighters closing in from astern and on both sides of the lead P-38, and Jordan seemed oblivious to Wire's cries over the radio for the two of them to rejoin their formation.

When two 'Oscars' rolled into a 'split-s' in an effort to trap Wire while he was separated from his leader, he decided on turning into the enemy fighters. The drill of never manoeuvring with Japanese fighters – especially when separated from other Americans – raced through Wire's mind as he pulled hard into the Ki-43s, but he felt that the situation demanded unconventional tactics. And this time it worked, as one of the 'Oscars' began

433rd FS P-38H '172' was parked on the runway at Dobodura during the Rabaul period in 1943 when it was rammed by a careening B-24, which took the Lightning's right wing outboard of the engine completely off and then left one of its propellers embedded in the fighter's right wing root (*Hanks*)

to fall apart when accurate fire from the P-38's concentrated nose guns hit it. The other Japanese pilot was apparently unnerved and flew away.

Jordan, meanwhile, had at last spotted Wire's predicament, and he joined up in time to discourage additional enemy fighters from closing on his tail. Wire took up his position on Jordan's wing, shooting at another 'Oscar' when the two Lightning pilots flew over the target area at just 4000 ft – he subsequently told the debriefing officer that he saw the Japanese fighter flying away trailing smoke. Minutes later, Wire heard over the radio that the bombers had dropped their loads on the target and were heading home, so both P-38 pilots decided to follow them back to base, with low fuel and ammunition as an added inducement to retreat.

2Lt John Smith (in P-38H-1 42-66538) was the only other 433rd FS pilot to score a kill during this particular mission when he claimed a 'Hamp' (actually a Ki-43) shot down and a twin-engined Ki-46 'Dinah' reconnaissance aircraft badly damaged.

Although he had previous combat experience flying reconnaissance missions in New Guinea, Smith was nominated by his squadronmates as being most likely to become a casualty because of his reckless attitude towards combat, and on this mission he almost fulfilled the prophecy.

Becoming separated after tangling with the Ki-43 and Ki-46, Smith soon lost his way whilst trying to get back to Dobodura. His compass was out, and the fix given to him by the Bena Bena radar station was not much help either. Afraid that he was flying into enemy territory, he made a 90-degree turn to the right and continued on until he was almost out of fuel. Smith crash-landed in a field just by the coast, being knocked senseless and suffering some cuts and bruises as the fighter ground to a halt. Later, he hiked to an Australian radio station at Siabai, which was not on the northern New Guinea coast, but across the bay from Port Moresby! He made it back to his base a few weeks later.

Incidentally, Smith's P-38 was recovered in 2005 from its final resting place and is now a possible candidate for restoration.

INTRUSION NORTHWARD

Allied pressure was now building against Japanese positions defending Lae and Salamaua, with Australian ground forces and American paratroopers threatening from the east and north. As part of the military build up in-theatre, radar stations had also been installed in places like Tsili Tsili and Bena Bena to give effective direction to the Allied air forces that would cover the invading convoys approaching from the sea off Lae in early September.

Maj Gen Kenney was confident that his forces could protect the vulnerable troop convoys, in spite of the fact that few replacement pilots or aircraft were available to make good any losses suffered in the immediate future. He also felt that the gamble he had taken in setting up the 475th FG as an elite unit had already paid off, and he stated that the standards set by the group in combat during its August engagements over Wewak were unmatched.

4 September saw heavy fighting over the invasion beaches in the Huon Gulf, on New Guinea's northern coast, and Maj Gen Kenney's impression of the quality apparent in his aircrews was reinforced during the day in spite of the successes achieved by determined Japanese air attacks.

The 475th FG experienced its first action at 1315 hrs, when P-38s of the 433rd FS were scrambled to join Lightnings from the 80th FS/8th FG and P-47s from the 39th FS/35th FG and the newly arrived 348th FG in response to a heavy Japanese bombing attack on the invasion convoy. By the end of the engagement several barges and beachheads had been hit, but the American fighters had accounted for 20 fighters and bombers shot down. Five of these victories were credited to the 475th, with two bombers and two fighters falling to pilots from the 433rd FS, and a Zero, according to official lists, being claimed by Col Prentice himself.

Capt Joe McKeon (in P-38H-1 42-66581) was an old hand in-theatre by the time he waded into the Japanese formations near Lae on 4 September. Indeed, he had been one of the pilots transferred from the 15th FG to the 8th FG in August 1942 following Maj Gen Kenney's call for additional pilots for V Fighter Command. Assigned to the 35th FS, McKeon had downed a Zero whilst flying P-39D-1 41-38353 over Buna on 7 December 1942 – a fitting way to mark the first anniversary of the Pearl Harbor attack. Transferred to the 475th FG in June 1943, and promoted to captain shortly afterwards, McKeon's after action report for 4 September read as follows;

'Three flights were scrambled on an alert at 1315 hrs. I was leading "Blue Flight" in trail of "Red" and "White", and once on course, we headed in a fast climb in the direction of Hopoi. We cut straight across the sea, and at an altitude of 15,000 ft, immediately across from Natter Bay, contacted the enemy attacking our shipping. Before reaching the vicinity, "Red" and

A Red Cross worker serves refreshments to pilots that have just returned from an operation. The latter are, from left to right, Col George Prentice, Maj Al Schinz, Capt Bill Haning and Maj Frank Nichols. 1Lt Phillips can be seen standing in the background (*Cooper*)

"White" flights initiated the attack, and from my position I couldn't distinguish the type and number of enemy aeroplanes. However, I saw two large puffs and trails of white smoke indicating destroyed aeroplanes, presumably enemy.

'On reaching the area, I attacked a group of fighters milling in a circle towards us. Singling one out, I hunted him down for a closing deflection shot, approaching from nearly head-on. He was seen to leave a huge trail of smoke by my wingman. With the exception of a few P-38s, the area was occupied by 30 or more enemy fighters. I circled and climbed outside the area, and then made a head-on pass at several flying at the same level. One made a half-hearted pass at myself and my wingman, who had stayed with me throughout the fight. As we closed to about 150 yards, he half rolled, straightened out and dove. I fired on him, pushing over at the same time to keep my sights on him – no results were observed.

'The preceding action took about 15 to 20 minutes. The area then cleared of all action, and after cruising around for an additional 30 minutes, I headed for home.'

2Lt Walter Reinhardt was flying on McKeon's wing, and he added some notes to the action from his perspective;

'After Capt McKeon's burst, the "Oscar's" engine caught on fire and smoked heavily. The "Oscar" went into a very steep dive from 14,000 ft. This "Oscar", in my estimation, was burning too much to ever reach its home base. He then made a pass on another "Oscar", firing from 100 yards down to 50 yards, without any results noticed. The enemy aeroplanes then left the area, and after circling we returned home. I got in two passes, but achieved no results. Both "Oscars" came at us head-on as we attacked, then peeled off. The "Oscars" did not seem to press home their attacks. After an attack, they peeled off and got out. I thought I saw one barge afire on the water below us.'

Following this clash, a lull fell over the Huon Gulf area during the next few weeks. A few Japanese raiders were claimed by patrols over the landing grounds, but the effectiveness of the fighter control system must have discouraged enemy interference with the operations to secure Lae. V Fighter Command instead turned its attention once more to Wewak, scheduling a series of bomber missions during which P-38 escorts from the 475th FG downed a number of Japanese fighters.

Future aces were amongst the pilots who enjoyed success over Wewak during September, with Capt Verl Jett claiming a 'Nick' and 2Lt Vincent Elliott an 'Oscar' (again claimed as a 'Zeke') on the 13th. The Ki-45 was Jett's fifth confirmed victory (his first had come in P-39D-1 41-38396 on 28 December 1942 whilst serving with the 36th FS/8th FG), whilst the Ki-43 was the first of seven for Elliott. 1Lt Warren Lewis got his second (of seven) when he claimed an 'Oscar' on 28 September, and 1Lt Tom McGuire claimed two more Ki-43s on the same day to raise his total to nine destroyed – once again, both pilots had stated that these aircraft were 'Zekes'.

Over in the 432nd FS, 2Lt Billy Gresham (in P-38H-1 42-66565) got two Ki-61s over Marilinan on 20 September for his second and third of six victories. And it was the 432nd FS that set a new record for the 475th over the Lae-Finschhafen invasion area when it tallied 18 victories for the loss of a single pilot on 22 September.

Capt Dennis Cooper, 475th FG
Intelligence Officer, presides over an
awards ceremony at Nadzab in early
1944 that honoured those that had
performed so valiantly during the
New Britain campaign in 1943.
Brig Gen Wurtsmith, Head of
V Fighter Command, would
present decorations to Maj Arsenio
Fernandez, Capt John Loisel
and 1Lts Paul Lucas and Art Peregoy
on this particular occasion (*Cooper*)

The Imperial Japanese Navy (IJN) had been largely ignoring New Guinea and focusing instead on what it considered to be the greater threat in the Solomons, but the loss of Lae-Salamaua and imminent assault on Finschhafen demanded some sort of response. It duly came in the form of G4M 'Betty' bombers from the 702nd and 751st Kokutais, covered by Zeros of the 201st, 204th and 253rd Kokutais, which were despatched on 21/22 September to find and attack the invasion convoys.

When the convoys were finally discovered on the morning of 22 September, a force of eight torpedo-armed 'Bettys' were sent off in three waves, covered by some 35 Zeros from the three fighter units. It was this force that was engaged by the 432nd, as well as other units, during the early afternoon of 22 September near the Finschhafen invasion area. The Allied fighter controller tracking the approaching Japanese formation gave the US pilots updated plots every five minutes until they finally spotted the enemy aircraft at about 6000 ft, their wings glistening through the broken clouds.

Capt Fred 'Squareloop' Harris (in P-38H-5 42-66869) was the high-scoring P-38 pilot for the day, and his after action report described his mission experiences on the 22nd;

'I saw six "Betty" bombers, with ten Zeros as close cover, and above us were 20 to 30 more Zeros as high cover, doing aerobatics. I immediately told the squadron to drop belly tanks, and we started down on the bombers, trying to head them off before they reached their target. During our dive, we attained a speed of 500 mph indicated. As we were approaching them they were also diving at a very high rate of speed, and they went under a thin layer of clouds, temporarily obliterating their whole flight. We went over the top of the thin layer of clouds and ended up right in the middle of their close cover, with their top cover hitting us from above. One of them got on my tail, pouring lead into me. My wingman, 2Lt Zach Dean (in P-38H-1 42-66504), shot the Zero off my tail – I saw it spin into the water.

'This attack split up the Zeros completely, and they left their bombers. This left 1Lt Ince's and 1Lt Loisel's flights with a clear pass at the bombers. Our second pass was made at three bombers that were off by themselves. On that pass we got two bombers – I got one which caught fire amidship and went right into the ocean, and my wingman, 2Lt Dean, hit a "Betty" to our left which apparently had not dropped its torpedo because the bomber exploded in mid-air.

'Following this attack, we gained a high rate of speed. As we could not see any more bombers, I peeled off after a Zero that was slightly lower and ahead of us. After I fired, he went straight into the ocean. We then climbed up for more altitude in search of more Zeros. We saw a few more Zeros floating around, but they were taken care of by P-38s and P-47s.

'At the time that the P-38s and P-47s were mixing it up with the enemy fighters, I saw four Zeros go down. I believe three were hit by the 39th FS and one by the P-47s. At this time I saw a straggler, very low, trying to sneak home. I roared up on him and shot him down. 2Lt John Rundell, who was in my second element, saw him crash after 2Lt Dean and I had passed by.

'We circled for about 15 minutes while "Duckbutt" (area fighter controller) searched for more Zeros. The controller then called us and said everything was okay. He next reported that pilots were down in rafts, so we went down to search the area. While we were searching, "Duckbutt" reported that 1Lt Vivian Cloud (in P-38H-1 42-66575) had been rescued and was okay. 2Lt Dean called me and said he was low on gas and out of ammunition, so we assembled our squadron and came home.'

Many 'Bettys' and Zeros were claimed, even though Japanese losses were limited to seven bombers shot down and an eighth that was forced to crash-land upon reaching its base, while at least eight fighters failed to return from the mission. American claims amounted to 40 Japanese

Pilots from the 432nd FS line up to receive their decorations at the same ceremony as seen on the opposite page. The men in the front row are, from left to right, Fernandez, Mann, Michener, Summer, Ilnicki, Ratajski and Noakes, whilst Hanson is having his decoration pinned on his chest by Brig Gen Wurtsmith. Capt Cooper is again at the microphone, and Col MacDonald can be seen standing in the foreground to the right (*Cooper*)

Two unidentified pilots from the 432nd FS conduct some 'hangar flying' for the benefit of the camera beneath 1Lt Ferdinand Hanson's P-38H *EL TORO* (*Author*)

aircraft shot down in total, giving some idea of the complexity and confusion surrounding this large engagement. Whatever the actual totals, the 432nd FS earned a record 18 confirmed claims for a single squadron in a single engagement, for the loss of two P-38s, with one of the pilots being recovered safely.

RABAUL

One of the key Japanese positions that threatened all Allied forces in the South and Southwest Pacific was the fortress of Rabaul, on the Gazelle peninsula of New Britain. Aircraft operating from airfields surrounding Rabaul could strike at Allied targets either in New Guinea or the Solomons, in addition to maintaining a position of key strategic defence for much of the Pacific theatre. The Japanese had put considerable effort into fortifying Rabaul, and the Allies knew full well that it would be a difficult nut to crack.

Gen Douglas MacArthur argued for the invasion of Rabaul, but most other Pacific strategists explained that sanity dictated such a formidable objective be isolated and bypassed. Privately, MacArthur was not keen on invading this Japanese fortress either, but publicly he felt he had to push for such an attack in order to build up his own case for the invasion of the Philippines, which was his primary strategic goal for the theatre.

Allied plans were to take enough territory such as the Admiralty Islands, in the nearby Bismarck Archipelago, in order to isolate Rabaul, and then bomb the existing forces on the airfields in the area, and in Rabaul's Simpson Harbour, to ineffectiveness. Every air commander wanted a crack at the place, so all units assigned to the Fifth and Thirteenth Air Forces, as well as Navy land- and carrier-based aircraft, were poised to attack.

Maj Gen Kenney again led the way by scheduling a bombing raid on 12 October 1943. Upwards of 200 B-24s and B-25s, joined by 16 Australian Beaufighters and an escort of more than 100 P-38s (including a provisional squadron), flew the 300+ miles to the airfields at Vunakanau and Kokopo (the latter called Rapopo in Allied contemporary reports for some unknown reason) and apparently caught the enemy completely by surprise.

The only fighter claim on the day was made by 1Lt John Fogarty of the 432nd FS, who was flying with the provisional squadron. The 432nd's war diary described the mission as follows;

'Today was the day that our pilots have been waiting many months for. The day when they would at last fly over the Japanese stronghold of Rabaul – 100 B-24s, 115 B-25s, 120 P-38s and 16 Beaufighters were to participate in the largest strike ever made against this Japanese base. Twenty of our aeroplanes took off at 0730 hrs to escort the fast-flying, strafing B-25s that were to sweep over Vunakanau and Rapopo airfields.

Maj Tompkins, 1Lts Hedrick and Wilson and Flt Off Ratajski were in "Red Flight", Capt Byers and 1Lts Hanson, Summer and Ritter flew in "Blue Flight", Capt Waldman and 1Lts Fostakowski, Gholson and Gresham made up "Green Flight" and 2Lts Farris and Lawhead made up the spares, with 1Lts McGuire and Fogarty flying in the provisional squadron.

'The strips at Vunakanau and Rapopo were strafed by the B-25s, and our fliers noticed several fires which might have been burning aircraft. The B-25s also strafed a "Sugar Charlie" and two barges. No interception of any kind was met. 1Lt Fogarty, flying in the provisional squadron, destroyed a stray "Betty" bomber after his flight leader, Maj Smith of Group Headquarters, made the initial pass. All aeroplanes stopped at Kiriwina for refuelling. All bar three returned to base at 1445 hrs. The three that remained did so because of small mechanical problems.

'Not a round of ammunition was expended, except by 1Lt Fogarty, but 36 belly tanks were dropped. Naturally, all of our pilots were disappointed because they didn't see combat, but they were well satisfied with the results of the mission. Maj Tompkins and Capt Harris were perturbed considerably because the Aussies broke radio silence en route to the target and the crews of the B-25s were guilty of the same act. Shortly after the mission had been completed, Capt Byers was hospitalised with possible malaria.'

Two small airstrips on the island of Kiriwina had been prepared as emergency refuelling depots for the P-38 escorts, and many aircrew owed their survival to these bare bases created at the north and south ends of the island to receive combat aircraft in need of fuel or repair.

1Lt Ferdinand Hanson was on hand in the 432nd FS at the time of the Rabaul raids, and he made some interesting notes in his diary about the value of Kiriwina, as well as the state of mind of some of the great American aces in-theatre;

'I remember that we are going to Rabaul in the morning. We have overnighted at Kiriwina so as to be closer to the target. We are standing around waiting at the ready shack for the signal to scramble. The 475th and other fighter groups are involved.

432nd FS pilot 1Lt Ferdinand C Hanson whimsically commented that he had several 'probable' victories – 'probably not'! (*Author*)

This unnamed, and clearly combat-weary, P-38H served with the 433rd FS in the final weeks of 1943 (*Author*)

'Capt Bong is in full flight gear, sitting on a stump or rock digging into the ground with his survival knife. He is "Mr Cool". Capt MacGuire is just the opposite. Man, he is nervous and jumpy. We all are. He is saying – "Let's get this show on the road – Now!" Dick Bong just looks up, grins a little and then continues digging into the ground. We later get the signal and we take off.'

JAPANESE RESPONSE

This first heavy raid on Rabaul demanded some sort of counter-blow from the Japanese, which was delivered quickly but without sufficiently heavy force on 15 and 17 October. The target hit was the critically important harbour facility at Oro Bay. This was used as a key staging point for Allied troops and equipment waging the offensive in New Guinea, and a concentrated blow here could have stalled the campaign in the Southwest Pacific for some considerable time.

Fifteen 'Val' dive-bombers of the 582nd Kokutai, escorted by 39 Zeros of the 204th Kokutai, took off from Rabaul in the early morning hours of 15 October to attack shipping in Oro Bay. Even with the improved warning network of radar stations and coast watchers, the force was able to penetrate deeply into Allied airspace, partly because they flew some of the way at lower altitude to avoid radar detection.

Amongst the men to enjoy success on this day was pre-war fighter pilot Maj Charles MacDonald, who had only joined the 475th FG two weeks earlier after completing a stint as CO of the P-47-equipped 340th FS/348th FG. Posted to the group's headquarters unit, he was just leaving the 475th's HQ building shortly before 0800 hrs on 15 October when Capt

Maj Charles MacDonald's first combat successes were scored on 15 October 1943 over Oro Bay in 2Lt Bud Wire's P-38H when he downed two 'Vals' moments after taking off. He was then set upon by the dive-bombers' escorts, forcing him to crash-land the badly damaged Lightning at Dobodura. MacDonald was reportedly in such good spirits at having escaped injury, as well as having claimed his first two victories, that he laughed wildly when he emerged from the broken cockpit. Bud Wire's reaction went unrecorded (*Hanks*)

Jesse Ivey drove up in a Jeep and excitedly told MacDonald that a Japanese bombing force was on its way in. The two officers tore off in the Jeep and were disappointed at first when they could find no P-38s in the 432nd's dispersal area. However, they soon came across two Lightnings that belonged to the 433rd FS, and MacDonald ordered Bud Wire's crew chief to get his P-38 (aircraft '193') ready for flight.

Wire himself got to the alert tarmac just as MacDonald and Ivey were taxiing across the airfield for the fastest possible take-off. The crew chief, who received some unremitting wrath from his pilot, told Wire that he was not going to argue with a headquarters major, leaving the future ace to watch in frustration as his P-38 took off to meet the enemy without him at the controls.

MacDonald did not even have time to raise his landing gear before he saw that he was going to cross flightpaths with the Japanese dive-bombers. Quickly shooting one down, he then lost Ivey when the latter went after several other 'Vals'. Another dive-bomber was destroyed by MacDonald, and two others were hit by his fire, before the Zero escort badly damaged his P-38. Although MacDonald was now far out to sea, and unable to spot any other friendly aircraft, he somehow managed to coax the damaged Lightning back to Dobodura, where he made a textbook wheels up crash-landing.

The mechanics who raced up to the battered P-38 as it steamed on the runway wondered at the major's sanity as he emerged from the shattered cockpit laughing maniacally at the thought of his narrow escape, as well as his initial claims as a fighter pilot in combat after four long years in the frontline.

Like Maj MacDonald, future ace 2Lt Frank Monk also enjoyed success for the first time over Oro Bay on 15 October 1943 when he claimed a Zero destroyed (*Author*)

Sixteen P-38Hs from the 433rd FS overfly Dobodura in tight four-ship formations. This was the ideal way to start and finish a mission (*Hanks*)

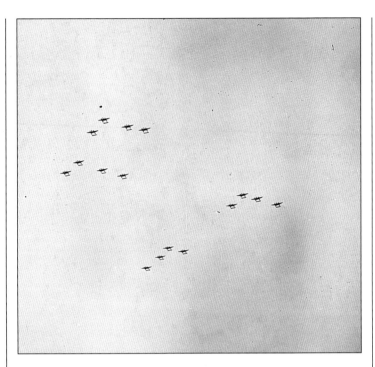

The most successful pilot to emerge from this action was 2Lt 'Fran' Lent (in P-38H-1 42-66550), who took off in the second element of the first 431st FS formation to depart Dobodura;

'We were scrambled from No 12 strip at 0810 hrs. I was leading the element in the first flight. We climbed to about 18,500 ft over Oro Bay, sighted the enemy and dropped our belly tanks. 1Lt Kirby (in P-38H-1 42-66593) dived down on a "Val" and I saw it burst into flames and fall into the water. I broke away and followed a second "Val" which was heading out to sea. I fired five bursts from approximately 500 ft, directly from the rear, and my fire was returned by the rear gunner. Then the "Val" burst into flames and crashed into the sea. This "Val" is confirmed by 2Lt Hedrick.

'At this time I saw two Zeros being followed by three P-38s, and I headed out to sea after them. Before I could catch up, both "Zekes" had burned and crashed. I then saw another "Val" about 1000 ft above the water, and as I attacked I was joined by a flight of three more P-38s. I fired a 90-degree deflection shot at this "Val" and missed. The other P-38s got him. I flew on out to sea looking for enemy aircraft, and spotted a "Zeke" heading for home, right down on the deck. Evidently, he didn't see me, because I got right on his tail and fired and he burst into flames and dropped into the water.

'After this I saw about three P-38s chasing two "Zekes" and I joined in this fight. One of the "Zekes" did a loop and a half-roll and I got a good deflection shot at him until I got on his tail and kept firing until he burst into flames. After this I was out of ammunition, so I headed home.'

By then the 432nd FS had also managed to break into the confused battle, and in just a matter of minutes its pilots accounted for six 'Vals', four Zeros and an 'Oscar' that had possibly blundered into the engagement. Capt John Loisel (in P-38H-1 42-66682) got two Zeros to

give him five confirmed victories overall, Capt Fred Harris (in P-38H-5 42-66832) also got two 'Vals' to take his tally to seven victories and 1Lt Frank Tompkins destroyed a Zero and a 'Val'.

Frustratingly for Bud Wire, he had missed the 433rd's best day so far, as his squadron claimed 15 fighters and dive-bombers, including the four racked up by MacDonald and Ivey. One of those to score a kill was Capt Joe McKeon (in P-38H-5 42-66856), who got a 'Val' to give him ace status.

Two days later, the Japanese again attempted to hit Oro Bay in much the same way that they had done on the 15th. A force of Zeros ranged out over the water towards the base from Rabaul, perhaps with nothing more in mind than to pick a fight with Allied aircraft. There is some evidence to suggest that seasoned pilots from the crack 253rd Kokutai were among the Zeros' pilots in action on this day. There is a chance that one of them might have been CPO Hiroyoshi Nishizawa, Japan's third-ranking ace of World War 2, who was flying with the 253rd Kokutai at the time this engagement took place.

At about 0930 hrs the alarm was sounded at Dobodura, and P-38s from the 431st and 433rd FSs were scrambled off airstrip No 12 to intercept the force that was reported to be approaching from the direction of Rabaul. Coincidentally, the 432nd FS was just returning from a mission to Lae at the time, and its pilots sighted the enemy formation off in the distance. However, a shortage of fuel demanded that they skirt around the Japanese fighters and land first in order to replenish their tanks.

For the 433rd FS, this would be the unit's first encounter with the enemy under the leadership of Capt Danny Roberts (in P-38H-5 42-66852), who had replaced Maj Low as CO on 3 October.

Capt Marion Kirby (in P-38H-5 42-66849) was leading the 431st at the head of 'Hades Red Flight', with 1Lt Kenneth Richardson as his

431st FS P-38 '136' was usually flown by Capt John Hood during the latter half of 1943

Capt Joe McKeon scored his first victory in a P-39D whilst flying with the 35th FS/8th FG in December 1942, then claimed four more kills with P-38s in the 433rd FS/475th FG and added a seventh victory in a P-51D when assigned to the 77th FS/20th FG in the UK in August 1944. McKeon's fifth confirmed kill was also scored during the 'Val' massacre over Oro Bay on 15 October 1943 (*Cooper*)

Future nine-kill ace 2Lt Fred Champlin of the 431st FS had his P-38H nosed over by 2Lt Pare upon the latter's return from the 17 October 1943 operation to Buna. The 'Hades' squadron lost two P-38s (and had this aircraft damaged) and a pilot during this mission, although eight Zeros were claimed to have been shot down in return (*Author*)

wingman, and 1Lt Edward Czarnecki (in P-38H-1 42-66592), with 2Lt Vincent Elliott (in P-38H-1 42-66550) as his wingman, in the second element. 'Red Flight' was patrolling between Tufi Point and Buna Point when the squadron ran head on into the Japanese formation. Kirby's after action report detailed his flight's engagement;

'We were at 22,500 ft when we saw about 20 "Zekes" at 20,000 ft, heading south-southwest. We circled and attacked from the rear. The flight I was leading attacked the foremost "Zekes". I fired at one on this pass but missed, or perhaps damaged it slightly. I then turned to my right (heading towards shore) and made a pass at a "Zeke" which three other P-38s were engaging. I made one pass and then turned to see 1Lt Czarnecki shoot the "Zeke" down. I then headed out to sea again and ran into a number of "Zekes" in a Lufbery circle. I made a pass on three of them, hitting one. 2Lt Elliott saw him go down. I then banked my aeroplane around and saw 2Lt Elliott hit one, which burst into flames almost immediately.

'I was looking for more aeroplanes when I saw a "Zeke" being chased by a number of P-38s. They all made a pass at it and the last one either got the "Zeke" or it fell to a lone P-40 that was sitting directly overhead the fighter as it came out of a "split-s" manoeuvre – I could not tell from my position. As the "Zeke" was going down, a parachute fell away from it, and as the parachute neared the water I noticed an aeroplane circling it. I thought it was yet another enemy aircraft, and I went to investigate it, but as I neared the 'chute I identified the circling fighter as friendly.

'By now I had gotten a long way away from the fight, and with my motors detonating at high manifold pressure, I decided not to rejoin the engagement. I duly returned to base.'

Czarnecki was credited with two Zeros destroyed following the fight, taking his tally to six kills overall. He was forced to bail out of P-38H-5 42-66849 over enemy territory six days later and spent three months evading capture until meeting up with other aircrew evaders and being rescued by a US submarine in February 1944.

The successes of 17 October meant that 'Red Flight' had accounted for four of the nine Zeros tallied by the 431st on this day. Three of the remaining five claims were submitted by 1Lt Tom McGuire (in P-38H-5 42-66836), but he nearly paid with his life for his daring attacks.

Maj Frank Nichols poses with his Lightning (P-38H-5 42-66836) sometime prior to the fighter being shot down with 1Lt Tom McGuire at the controls on 17 October 1943 (*Cooper*)

Capt Verl Jett's P-38H is seen here after its squadron number had been changed from '120' to '110' to signify his assuming command of the 431st FS on 22 November 1943 (*Author*)

Among the positive things to be said about McGuire amid claims that he was reckless and overbearing is the fact that he was a consistent team player who scrupulously followed the policies of his unit, and service in general. In this fight, he was responsible for saving the life of a fellow pilot with such utter disregard to his own safety that he was himself shot down into the sea.

The first of his three victories for the day was observed by Navy Corpsman Arthur Kemp and Marine Corps TSgt J B Pruett. McGuire had scrambled at the head of 'White Flight', with 2Lt Hunt again on his wing, when the P-38 pilots ran straight into the enemy formation. Kemp and Pruett were watching the progress of the battle through field glasses, and later jointly signed the following statement;

'On 17 October 1943, I was watching the aerial combat which took place over Buna Bay. I was standing on the beach looking through field glasses, and had a clear view of the combat. At the beginning of the combat I saw two P-38s attack a "Zeke". One of the P-38s pulled away, but the other one followed the "Zeke" down, firing several bursts, until he too broke away. This second P-38 was the one piloted by 1st Lt Thomas B McGuire, Jnr, and I saw the "Zeke" on which 1Lt McGuire fired go down smoking and explode just before it hit the water.'

McGuire kept diving in and out of the fight, shooting or dodging the fire from the Zeros behind him. He observed one P-38 in apparent mortal danger with two Zeros behind him. Despite McGuire being the target of seven more enemy fighters, he took a 90-degree deflection shot at one of the Zeros menacing his squadronmate and it burst into flames. The ace then closed in on the tail of the second enemy fighter and set this aircraft alight too after opening fire from close range.

By now the seven Zeros immediately behind McGuire were in a perfect position to inflict telling damage on the latter's Lightning – this aircraft was actually assigned to Maj Frank Nichols, since McGuire had yet to receive a replacement for 42-66592, which had been written off in combat on 29 August. The Japanese fighters wrecked the P-38's left engine and damaged the right one, as well as shooting out the radio immediately behind the pilot. Shrapnel from the latter hits wrecked the cockpit and wounded McGuire in the arm, wrist and backside.

Destined for yet another bomber escort mission, P-38Hs from the 432nd FS taxi past stationary Lightnings from the 433rd FS at an unidentified airstrip during the Rabaul campaign (*Author*)

1Lt Clifford J Mann of the 432nd FS claimed a Zero probably destroyed over Rabaul on 24 October 1943, and followed this up with a confirmed victory in 1944 (*Hoxie*)

Capt Danny Roberts was assigned this particular P-38H-5 (42-66752) during his 37 days in charge of the 433rd FS in October-November 1943. He claimed three 'Zekes' destroyed over Rabaul with the aircraft on 23-24 October – he was also awarded a probable 'Zeke' kill in the fighter on 2 November. Although Roberts' own score was officially limited to 14 at the time of his death in action, his squadron had claimed an impressive 55 victories during his brief period in command (*Author*)

Desperately fighting for his life, McGuire dived away, knowing full well that he would have to abandon the aeroplane. He ripped himself free of the jagged cockpit and managed to open his parachute, despite its D-ring handle having been shot away. Now free of his stricken fighter, McGuire floated the short distance down into the water.

Despite being wounded, and bobbing around in a partly-inflated, bullet-damaged, raft in shark-infested waters, McGuire was more concerned about what his commander was going to say to him in respect to the loss of his aeroplane than about his imminent rescue. That rescue did come about 45 minutes later when PT boat No 152 plucked the ace from the water. McGuire's luck even extended to the fact that his rescuers had watched the last part of the fight, and Lt George Westfeldt signed another statement verifying that the second pair of Zeros engaged by McGuire had indeed crashed into the sea.

Despite the successes of the 431st FS on 17 October, for once the unit's exploits were overshadowed by the 433rd FS thanks primarily to the efforts of new CO, Capt Danny Roberts (who claimed two 'Zekes' with

432nd FS pilots 1Lts Bob Kimball and Art Peregoy pose outside their tent in late 1943. Peregoy had two confirmed kills to his name by the end of that year, and Kimball claimed three victories in the Philippines in 1944 (*Hoxie*)

P-38H-5 42-66852). Since transferring in from the 432nd FS, he had been instilling the concept of teamwork into his charges, telling his pilots to 'hunt like a pack of wolves'. This idea so inspired the unit that it claimed ten Zeros for the loss of just one P-38 and its pilot. The 431st had also suffered a single fatality, but had been fortunate in having Tom McGuire returned so expeditiously to the fold. Thus, for the net loss of two pilots and three Lightnings, the 475th FG had added an impressive 19 victories to its tally.

As for Maj Frank Nichols, he took the loss of his P-38 with equanimity since his squadron had now claimed more than 65 victories in just two months of operations, and Tom McGuire had become the leading ace in theatre with 13 kills. Also, Nichols was virtually tour expired, expecting to turn his squadron over to Operations Officer Verl Jett by the end of the next month.

Despite these attacks on Oro Bay, the Allied offensive against Rabaul went on, and weather conditions permitted a high-level bombing mission by B-24s on 23 October. Ten of the approximately thirteen claims submitted in the wake of this mission were made by the 475th FG, with the 433rd FS being credited with four of them. Capt Roberts (flying P-38H-5 42-66752) once again led the way with two 'Zekes' to boost his tally to 11 kills.

It was the duty of the 433rd FS on this mission to sweep ahead of the bombers and clear away any enemy fighters that were attempting to hinder the B-24s' progress to the target. Roberts related the details of his engagements with the Zeros in his after action report;

'We reached the target area a little early, so we made several circuits outside before entering the target area, at 1215 hrs. Several Zeros were observed at 15,000 ft in the centre of the harbour, and approximately ten single-engined aeroplanes were between Rapopo and Vunakanau. Twelve Zeros headed out over the water toward Kavieng, but they then turned back and climbed up into our area.

'For several minutes, the two squadrons charged with providing the B-24s with low cover were sufficient in number to adequately take care of the Zeros. However, about 15 enemy fighters then appeared, so our squadron dropped its belly tanks and dived down from 25,000 ft to 20,000 ft. My radio messages were not received by the balance of my squadron, however, and as a result, two of the flights stayed too high, with only "Red" and "White Flights" going down.

'One flight from the 431st FS delivered an attack on approximately eight Zeros, and when several of the enemy pursued them, I flew directly behind a "Zeke", giving him three short bursts. As the "Zeke" turned right, I fired another burst, which left his left wing very ragged and the aeroplane burning furiously. I then

Pilots enjoy a drink at the Dobodura officers' club in late 1943. The 431st's 2Lt Pappy Cline is the tall officer standing to the left in the photograph, whilst squadronmate, and ace, 1Lt Jack Mankin is standing at the bar wearing a flying jacket and baseball cap (*Author*)

This dramatic still taken from the gun camera cine film of a V Fighter Command P-38 reveals a familiar sight for 475th FG pilots in the final months of 1943 – a Zero in a head-on attack (*USAF*)

executed an attack on another "Zeke" from a quarter head-on, firing a long burst. The "Zeke" immediately burned, rolled over and some large object appeared to drop from the cockpit. However, I saw no parachute open. This action took place at 19,000 ft. The Nips half-rolled when being attacked. We were too high to do effective work.'

This was the most intensive phase of the escorted bombing campaign against Rabaul, with another low altitude mission being flown the very next day. The low-level raids flown by B-25s and covered by P-38s were usually the most effective, as they elicited the greatest response from the Japanese.

24 October 1943 proved to be yet another fruitful day for the Lightning escorts, who claimed 40 Japanese aircraft shot down, including 12 for the 80th FS/8th FG and 18 for the 475th FG.

On 25 October the B-24s were again unleashed on Rabaul in a high altitude mission, but on this occasion the often treacherous weather in the area served the target well, as it forced most of the P-38 escorts to turn back before reaching the objective. In point of fact, only seven Lightnings from the 432nd FS, led by Maj Charles MacDonald, managed to stay with bombers from the 43rd and 90th BGs long enough to protect them from interception.

It was a peculiarity of this mission that Japanese records supported the single fighter claim made by Maj MacDonald (his fourth kill) and

1Lt Marion Kirby's P-38H-5 42-66827 was nicknamed *MAIDEN HEAD Hunter*, and it is seen here being serviced following the fighter's eventful 2 November 1943 mission to Rabaul. Kirby was so tense when his unit (431st FS) was taxiing out at the start of that mission that he cracked the glass on a cockpit instrument when he tap-tested it! Dubbed 'a real tiger' by his squadronmates both in the 80th and 431st FSs, Kirby claimed two 'Zekes' on the 2nd to take his final score to exactly five kills and one probable. His extended tour of duty ended in December 1943, at which point Kirby returned home with 126 combat missions to his name (*Tabatt*)

credited to the P-38 escort on this date. Those records admit to the loss of two 'Zeke' fighters, one of which fell to bomber gunners and the other to the escort, during an interception that was not pressed home with determination.

2Lt Zach Dean (who had claimed two kills in P-38H-1 42-66504 the previous day to 'make ace') was flying on MacDonald's wing, and he reported witnessing his leader's victory;

'The ack-ack was surprisingly accurate, bursting right at our level, which at this time was 28,000 ft. It is my belief that they had Zeros calling in our altitude. I saw about eight or ten enemy aircraft at our altitude, or slightly above. One of these foolishly tried to make a pass on seven of us unaided. Maj MacDonald made a beautiful deflection shot and the Nip exploded in mid-air. His complete tail assembly flew to pieces and burned furiously.'

Despite poor weather closing down operations against Rabaul for the next few days, Maj Gen Kenney was ecstatic over what he perceived to be the trouncing that his air forces were giving the enemy fortress. In point of fact, only modest damage had been inflicted on the area, and the Japanese quickly repaired their facilities. Indeed, Rabaul would continue to be an effective roadblock to Allied advances in the region for the rest of the year.

Maj Gen Kenney's view that the defenders of Rabaul were now a spent force was challenged on 29 October 1943, when a high altitude raid by B-24s against Vunakanau provoked only a fierce response from Japanese fighters. The 431st and 432nd FSs escorted the 'heavies', losing 2Lt Christopher Bartlett from the latter unit to either flak or enemy aircraft. The latter also forced 2Lt Robert 'Pappy' Cline to land at Kiriwina with approximately 30 bullet holes in his P-38.

The star performers once again were the pilots of the 433rd FS, ten of whom dived down from 28,000 ft over the target to engage an estimated 35 to 40 enemy interceptors harassing the bombers from below. With such numerical inferiority, it was necessary for the Lightning pilots to use conservative tactics, being content to simply divide the attention of the attacking enemy fighters rather than seeking out individual kills.

Nevertheless, six Japanese interceptors were claimed destroyed, including a 'Zeke' credited to Capt Danny Roberts (in P-38H-1 42-66574) for his 13th victory. 2Lt John Smith (in P-38H-1 42-66533) also downed a 'Zeke' for his sixth, and final, kill – he would perish in action over Alexishafen in P-38H-1 42-66538 11 days later.

1Lt John Babel was at the head of his flight as they dived into the massed ranks of Zeros, and his element leader, 1Lt Donald King recorded their successes in his after action report;

'As the bombers were withdrawing after finishing their run, we peeled off in pairs and engaged the 35-40 "Zekes", "Oscars" and "Tonys" that were circling loosely through the area at about 18,000 ft, attempting to intercept bombers from below. I followed my flight leader, 1Lt Babel, on one deflection pass at a "Zeke", and was about to follow him on another pass when a "Zeke" came down upon us from above and to the left at "eight o'clock high". I wheeled up into him and fired from 200 yards, head-on. We closed very fast, and the "Zeke" clipped my wingtip as he passed by. The "Zeke" was smoking very heavily and went down, followed by 1Lt Babel. The "Zeke" crashed into the ground smoking without having burst into flames. I received no injuries, but the wingtip of my aeroplane was damaged and must be replaced.

'The enemy pilots were better than usual today. They were wary, but fearless once they began a pass on a P-38.'

Other Lightning squadrons from V Fighter Command were credited with a dozen more claims, and Maj Gen Kenney was satisfied that the

These 432nd FS P-38Hs were photographed in the tree-lined squadron dispersal area at Dobodura in late October 1943. Aircraft '149' was assigned to newly-arrived 2Lt Joe Forster, who had joined the squadron from the 329th FG that same month. He would claim nine aerial victories whilst flying with the 432nd FS (Author)

Japanese air forces in the Rabaul area must have been badly crippled following this engagement. He would get the shock of his life four days later.

On 2 November weather conditions finally allowed another massive escorted raid to be undertaken, and Maj Gen Kenney hoped that this would knock out any remaining air power defending Rabaul. The mission called for 75 P-38s to escort B-25s to Simpson Harbour, where the latter would bomb and strafe whatever shipping was present. What the escorting P-38 pilots did not know was that the fighter units in the immediate area had not only made good their losses, they had been bolstered by reinforcements flown in from aircraft carriers or on temporary deployment from Japanese Army Air Force (JAAF) units in the surrounding areas.

The 431st FS bore the brunt of the action when its Lightnings entered the harbour area at 1340 hrs on the 2nd. As the unit's nine P-38s headed up the Warangoi River towards the harbour itself, they were fired on by destroyers anchored in its mouth. Having been bracketed by heavy flak, the 431st's flights had been forced to loosen their formations, thus making them vulnerable to attack by Japanese fighters. Sure enough, as they raced over the harbour at 2000 ft, the P-38 pilots spotted enemy interceptors diving down on them from 6000 ft. A wild fight ensued, with the Lightning pilots striving to defend themselves and the bombers.

1Lt Art Wenige (in P-38H-1 42-66511) was leading 'White Flight', and he claimed two 'Zekes' destroyed to take his overall tally to five kills. His wingman, 2Lt Frank Monk (in P-38H-1 42-66592), who also claimed a 'Zeke' for his second confirmed victory, described the encounter in the following after action report;

'We followed the bombers as they went across the beach at Cape Gazelle, at which point we were attacked by approximately 60 to 70 enemy aircraft. Moments later I saw 2Lt Lent (in P-38H-1 42-66550) shoot down a "Zeke", which burned and then crashed. The enemy aircraft dived down to attack both us and the bombers, and we engaged the enemy to divert their attention away from the B-25s.

'While 1Lt Lutton (in P-38H-5 42-66821) was engaged in destroying a "Zeke", which I saw crash in flames, he was attacked from behind by two more "Zekes". 1Lt Wenige attacked one of the enemy aircraft and I attacked the other "Zeke". I saw the "Zeke" that 1Lt Wenige was shooting at spin down out of control and crash into the sea. I fired a long burst at the other "Zeke", but it broke away and I did not see the results of my fire. We made many passes on enemy aircraft that were diving on 1Lt Lutton, 1Lt Wenige and myself. 1Lt Wenige fired at one of them which I saw burst into flames and explode. I fired a short burst at the other "Zeke", but did not see any damage.

'Another "Zeke" attacked us from above at approximately "one o'clock". 1Lt Wenige ducked under him and turned left, and I fired a burst into the "Zeke" and saw it start to burn. 1Lt Wenige saw this "Zeke" go down in flames and crash. Again seeing two "Zekes" diving on 1Lt Lutton, 1Lt Wenige and I dived on them. The two "Zekes" broke away and I got in a short burst, but saw no results.

'At this time there were approximately five or six enemy aircraft above and on both sides of us. One of those on the right made a diving attack and

2Lt Don King of the 433rd FS exults after a successful mission. A well-liked member of the 'Possum' squadron, he had claimed four Japanese fighters destroyed prior to his death in combat during the 'Bloody Tuesday' mission to Rabaul on 2 November 1943. Three other pilots from the 475th FG also perished on this day (*Hanks*)

1Lt Paul Morriss' P-38H-5 42-66826 *"Hold Everything"* has its artwork applied soon after the future five-kill ace used the fighter to claim his first two kills in late 1943. Morriss claimed three more victories in June 1944 with later model Lightnings to achieve ace status (*Author*)

passed within 50 ft of us. This was the last pass made at us by enemy aircraft. We were over the mouth of Wide Bay by this time, and continued on our way to Kiriwina.'

1Lt Marion Kirby (in P-38H-5 42-66827) was leading the 431st FS's 'Red Flight' on 2 November, and he shot down two 'Zekes' to take his finally tally to five kills. One of these aircraft was almost certainly being flown by 11-kill Zero ace Lt Yoshio Fukui. Several P-38 pilots reported seeing a Zero move in to finish off a B-25 and then be shot down by Kirby. Although suffering from burns, Fukui survived the encounter by parachuting from his blazing fighter at low altitude.

Thirteen 432nd FS P-38 pilots split up into three 'Clover' flights followed the 431st FS into the dogfight over Rabaul, and they too were forced to scrap for their lives just as the 'Hades' flights had done minutes earlier. 1Lt Grover Gholson (in P-38H-5 42-66832) had led the unit into battle, and he soon succeeded in latching onto the tail of an 'Oscar' long enough to send it down in flames. Minutes later he destroyed a Zero for his fifth, and final, victory since arriving in New Guinea in May 1942 – he had claimed his first kill (also a Zero) on 14 May 1942 whilst flying P-39Fs with the 36th FS/8th FG.

Six Japanese interceptors were claimed in total by the 432nd, including a 'Tony' for 2Lt Leo Mayo. Unfortunately, Mayo pressed home his attack to such an extent that a large chunk of the Ki-61's wing broke off and mortally damaged his P-38. Seen to bail out just offshore and last observed walking into the jungle, Mayo was never seen again.

The 433rd FS also got into an inconclusive scrap on the 2nd, with probable victories being awarded to Capt Danny Roberts (in P-38H-5 42-66752) and 1Lt Donald Revenaugh. 2Lt Donald King, who had claimed his fourth aerial victory on 29 October, was posted missing in the wake of this mission.

Although the 431st FS had made the most claims with nine confirmed kills, it had also suffered the most casualties with two pilots missing. 1Lt Kenneth Richardson went down near Rabaul, while 1Lt Lowell Lutton, who had just claimed his fifth victory, was spotted joining up at the tail end of 1Lt Wenige's 'White Flight' as it left the target area, but he then disappeared sometime after clearing Simpson Harbour. Postwar, in

The 432nd FS's 1Lt Jim 'Impossible' Ince claimed his last victories in this aircraft (P-38H-1 42-66568) on 9 and 16 November 1943, thus taking his final tally to six kills. His fifth victory (an 'Oscar', which Ince claimed as a 'Zeke') came during the same mission to Alexishafen in which Capt Danny Roberts was killed (*Ince*)

433rd FS groundcrews pose on one of their many charges at Dobodura in between missions in late 1943 (*Gallagher*)

November 1948, Art Wenige made this statement about Lutton's loss;

'Again and again on the 2 November mission 1Lt Lutton was singled out for attack by two or three enemy fighters at a time, and he was saved from destruction only by the valiant efforts of other members of the squadron. Despite this, 1Lt Lutton continued to lead his men in passes at the enemy aircraft attacking the bombers, thus showing that he had his squadron's focus and cohesion uppermost in his mind throughout the action.

'On the return flight to base, 1Lt Lutton lost his squadron in the overcast and a storm which barred the way back to Kiriwina from Rabaul. Unable to reach Kiriwina, 1Lt Lutton crashed into the ocean, and although a search was made, no trace of him was ever found.

'To the best of my knowledge, 1Lt Lutton's P-38, having been hit repeatedly by enemy fire over Wide Bay, went into an extremely shallow dive, struck the surface of the water and sank about 50 to 100 miles southwest of Rabaul.'

Fellow 431st pilot 2Lt Owen Giertson enjoyed better luck, however, for after he was shot down during the engagement, he managed to meet up with squadronmate 1Lt Ed Czarnecki. As previously mentioned, the latter pilot had survived a dunking in the same area on 23 October, and both men evaded capture until collected by the Allies and transported to Open Bay, on the northwest side of the Gazelle peninsula. From here, they were eventually picked up by submarine in February 1944.

Although both men survived their ordeals and were sent home, Czarnecki was subsequently plagued by ill health after he contracted a tropical disease whilst evading in New Britain. He eventually succumbed to tuberculosis in 1976 following three decades of deteriorating health.

Sgt Carl A King of the 431st FS made the following entry in his journal after the 2 November mission;

'1Lt Morriss "Snafu" in "120" (the P-38 serviced by King for Capt Verl Jett) from a Rabaul mission. We got into them and got nine, lost three including 1Lts Richardson and Lutton. That makes 74 Nips shot down.'

CHANGES

Two new squadron commanders and a new group CO changed the face, but not the spirit, of the 475th FG in the weeks following the

2 November mission. Sgt King again recorded events in his journal when Maj Frank Nichols left the 431st FS on 19 November 1943;

'We had got the troublesome right engine in "120" all ready to come out when up walked the group CO, who told us not to pull it. I wish they would make up their minds! Maj Nichols then told us that he was going home, and that Capt Jett – my pilot – would be our next CO. Later that day we all went over to the visiting USO show and saw Gary Cooper, Una Merkel and Phyllis Brooks in person.'

Change of command for the 433rd FS was a more sombre affair. Capt Danny Roberts had been in charge of the unit for a mere 37 days when he led the 9 November 1943 mission to Alexishafen, situated on the north New Guinea coast. Flying P-38H-5 42-66834, he had just claimed an 'Oscar' at low altitude (originally listed as a 'Hamp') for his 14th victory, and was chasing another, when he made a sudden turn that caused him to collide with his wingman, 2Lt Dale Meyer. Both men perished in the subsequent crash, and as previously mentioned, six-kill ace 2Lt John Smith was also shot down in the same area on the same mission to give the squadron one of its grimmest days in World War 2. Mild-mannered future ace

P-38H-5 42-66817 *PUDGY II* has its right engine changed in late December 1943. This aircraft served with the 431st FS from September 1943 until it was replaced by a P-38J-15 in early 1944 – a long time for a frontline fighter (*Author*)

Lt Col Charles MacDonald is seen here with his Supply Officer, Maj Claude Stubbs, soon after the former became group CO in November 1943 (*Author*)

Capt Warren Lewis took over command of the 433rd, and he led it until he was declared tour-expired in August 1944.

Maj Charles MacDonald (in P-38H-5 42-66846), who claimed two 'Zekes' in the same engagement to take his overall tally to five kills, witnessed the aftermath of the collision between Roberts and Meyer. Within three weeks MacDonald would replace Prentice as CO of the 475th FG, thus changing the group's style of leadership – MacDonald was a truly great fighter leader in the air – but not its primary focus of protecting Allied bombers or hunting down enemy aircraft. MacDonald would lead from the front and eventually become the only other pilot besides Tom McGuire and Dick Bong in the Southwest Pacific to surpass the mythical 26-victory mark of World War 1 ace Eddie Rickenbacker.

Men like Lewis and MacDonald would ensure that the 475th FG's valiant legacy would go on despite the terrible losses inflicted on the group in the final months of 1943.

That unlikely legacy went a long way to convincing Maj Gen Kenney that he was right to remain on the offensive, even though his pugnacious spirit had been shaken by recent events in-theatre. He was now ready to implement the Allied grand plan for the Southwest Pacific theatre by attacking strategic points along New Britain's southern coast, as well as outlying positions in the Rabaul salient. Kenney's ideas on strategy had not fulfilled his most sanguine hopes to date, but even doubters in other commands had to be impressed with the adverse effect the campaign in the New Britain and New Ireland areas was having on Japanese forces in the Solomons and Central Pacific.

For the rest of November, the 475th FG continued to fly bomber escort missions, covering 'heavies' sent to attack Rabaul on the 11th and Wewak five days later. Maj Meryl Smith (in P-38H-1 42-66682) from group HQ claimed two 'Zekes' (actually Ki-43s) during the latter operation for his

The Lightning in the foreground of this photograph is P-38G-13 43-2280, which returned early to Dobodura from the 16 December 1943 mission to New Britain with 432nd FS pilot 2Lt George Beatty at the controls. The other fighter is almost certainly P-38G-5 42-12644, flown by the 432nd's 1Lt Howard Hedrick, who had aborted the mission in order to provide Beatty with an escort. Hedrick claimed four aerial victories and one probable during his tour with the 475th FG (*Gallagher*)

first of nine victories, although three 431st P-38s failed to return from the mission after the squadron was jumped by an estimated 30 Japanese fighters. Two of the pilots were eventually recovered, but 1Lt Robert Smith was apparently killed in action. The group's two other squadrons claimed a pair of enemy fighters in return.

By the time the Fifth Air Force assault on Rabaul had ended, the Marine Corps had landed on Bougainville, in the Solomon Islands, and seized Cape Torokina after bitter fighting. Thanks to these successes, the Thirteenth Air Force now had airstrips within 250 miles of Rabaul, allowing it to take the fight directly to the Japanese fortress.

In December the Allies made a direct land assault on New Britain when 3000 troops of the 112th Cavalry Regiment landed on the Arawe peninsula during the morning of the 15th. Numerous diversionary and support attacks were carried out by both American and Australian aircraft over the next few days, and the 475th enjoyed its most successful period in combat since the Rabaul raids when it patrolled over Arawe on 16 December.

Poor weather initially delayed the 432nd from taking off on a B-24 escort to Cape Gloucester until 1230 hrs. About 90 minutes later, one flight was sent up to 24,000 ft to investigate unidentified aircraft, whereupon its pilots found 30 to 40 'Oscars' and 'Tonys' covering seven

1Lt Ritter's P-38 is seen here about to land on one of Dobodura's airstrips in December 1943. Ritter, of the 432nd FS, often flew as Lt Col MacDonald's wingman (*Gallagher*)

Lunch out on the line for the 431st FS in late 1943. Seated on the far side of the table, from left to right, are 1Lts Bill O'Brien, Fred Champlin, 'Pappy' Cline, Kidd, 'Fran' Lent, Robert Donald and Cortner, and on the near side, again from left to right, are 1Lts Wilson Ekdahl, Vincent Elliott and Paul Morriss. Four of these pilots became aces with a combined total of 32 kills between them (*Cooper*)

2Lt John Tilley scored his first victory for the 431st FS on 16 December 1943 when he downed a Ki-49 'Helen' bomber – quite possibly this very aircraft – near Arawe. This kill came just days after he had joined the unit (*Author*)

Groundcrewmen prepare Capt Tom McGuire's long-lived *PUDGY II* for its next mission in late 1943 (*Author*)

Ki-49 'Helen' heavy bombers. Continuing their climb in order to have the advantage of height, the 'Clover' squadron P-38s eventually fell on the Japanese escorts and drove them down to the same altitude as the bombers, claiming one of the 'Oscars' as damaged in the process.

At about this time the 431st showed up and attacked the bombers before they could escape into cloud. 1Lt David Allen led the squadron into the action, and as he pulled up after making his first pass, he noticed that there were still five Japanese bombers in formation trying to reach cloud. He fired at one on the outside right and saw pieces fly off before he had to break away beneath his target to avoid colliding with it. 2Lt Bill O'Brien was flying behind Allen, and he saw the 'Helen' (misidentified as a 'Betty') burst into flames, fall away and crash.

1Lt 'Fran' Lent attacked another bomber head on and watched as pieces flew off from the canopy area. Squadronmate 1Lt Carl Houseworth, who had led the flight down in the attack, was able to see the aircraft drop away trailing smoke. Lent erroneously claimed a 'Betty' destroyed, and was awarded a kill to take his tally to ten victories. Future five-victory ace 2Lt John Tilley, who had only joined the unit a matter of days earlier, also attacked the bombers and watched one go down in flames after he broke off his pass.

Now fully recovered from his wounds of 17 October, newly-promoted Capt Tom McGuire was back in action during this engagement, although he suffered from his usual problem of sighting the enemy in time to allow him to effect an attack. A number of his compatriots in V Fighter Command had been relieved when McGuire was confined to a hospital bed, for it meant that the air waves had been free of his incessant chattering as he called for the location of enemy aircraft. The ace was obsessed with locating Japanese aircraft once contact had been made by Allied units so that he could participate in the fighting.

On 16 December McGuire arrived too late to attack the bombers before they had reached the cloud cover, but he did manage to hit one of the 'Oscars' (he reported it as a 'Zeke') with a few bullets before it, too, escaped – he was credited with having damaged the aircraft.

The 433rd FS also tangled with the enemy on the 16th, Capt Warren Lewis leading from the front by claiming two 'Bettys' (actually Ki-49s) before they could reach cloud cover. Two more Ki-49s and a pair of Ki-43s were also claimed by the 'Possum' squadron to give the 475th credit for all seven bombers and at least two of the fighters downed during the engagement.

TSgt Ted Hanks, who was crew chief for Capt Danny Roberts' P-38, took this photograph from the safety of a ditch at Dobodura in order to avoid being hit by exploding ammunition. The grass fire raging in the background had been set intentionally by a clean up crew, but the controlled burn off soon got out of hand. The fighter in the foreground was one of the first J-model Lightnings to reach the 475th FG in December 1943 (*Hanks*)

1943 ended spectacularly for the entire Fifth Air Force when the 1st and 5th Marine Divisions invaded the Cape Gloucester area of northwest New Britain on 26 December 1943. Fighting over the southeastern corner of the island had also been heavy in the wake of the Arawe landings on 15 December, with all Lightning and Thunderbolt pilots involved finding opportunity to increase their scores.

The Marine Corps had seized control of several airstrips in the Cape Gloucester area by the afternoon of 29 December, these having been targeted by Japanese forces desperate to repel the invaders during the previous 72 hours – both the JAAF and IJN sortied aircraft against the invasion beaches and shipping offshore.

Three squadrons of P-47s, two of P-38s and another of P-40s countered enemy attacks during the afternoon of the 26th, claiming more than 60 aircraft – mostly Zeros and 'Vals' – shot down. Japanese records are obscure for the day, but they do reflect the loss of a number of 'Helen' and 'Val' aircraft, as well as fighters.

Capt Tom McGuire led the 431st FS into the fight, with the redoubtable 1Lt Frank Monk on his wing. The fighter controller handling the interception ordered the P-38s of the 80th PS/8th FG and 431st FS to attack a formation of enemy aircraft detected coming in from the northeast. The Lightning pilots were instructed to ignore the bombers and go after their fighter cover at 22,000 ft, so McGuire took his squadron up to 23,000 ft before engaging them head on.

For some reason the unit tasked with intercepting the 'Vals' below the Zeros was late in arriving, leaving the dive-bombers in a perfect position to attack the shipping off the coast just as McGuire dived down on their fighter escorts. The latter could clearly see the Aichi aircraft through the formation of Zeros, so he ordered his squadron to ignore the fighters and to intercept the 'Vals' instead.

In the wild manoeuvring which ensued, Monk lost his flight leader, but tacked onto the wing of an 80th FS P-38 engaging the Zeros. One fighter went down in smoke and flame after Monk's pass, and McGuire looked back to see the Japanese fighter crash into the sea.

'Hades White Flight' ran into 'Oscars' below the Zero cover and 1Lt Vince Elliott shot one of them down, as well as a Navy fighter, for his final

Groundcrewmen work on their fighters out in the open on the 431st FS maintenance line at Dobodura in late 1943. P-38H-5 '111' was usually flown by seven-kill ace 1Lt Vincent Elliott (*Author*)

confirmed victories (his tally now stood at seven kills). Capt Verl Jett, who was leading 'White Flight', also managed to damage a solitary 'Val'.

2Lt Herman Zehring, who was also a part of 'White Flight', experienced a great deal of difficulty in releasing one of his drop tanks, but he nevertheless managed to engage the 'Vals' and score his first two (of four) victories;

'I heard Capt McGuire say "Let's get the dive-bombers!" I then peeled off and followed my leader down. As I lost altitude, I saw the "Zeke" that 1Lt Monk had hit burst into flames and crash into the sea off Gloucester strip. When I was about 1000 ft above the water I came upon a "Val" type aircraft and fired a short burst which caused it to burst into flames and explode. 2Lt Powell saw it, too. After this, I caught a "Val" heading out, down near the water. I gave it a burst and the dive-bomber crashed into the water. 1Lt Elliott saw this aeroplane crash. After this, I couldn't find any more enemy aeroplanes, so I returned to base, where I landed at 1630 hrs.'

McGuire became wild in the midst of the 'Vals', which were disrupted by the American attacks to the point that only one hit was scored on a US Navy destroyer, which sank a few minutes later. At least seven 'Vals' were claimed by the 431st and two by P-47s of the 36th FS/8th FG, plus several others were listed as probably destroyed or damaged.

McGuire, himself, caused one to explode in mid-air, and watched three others hit the water following his attacks – one of these kills was eventually credited to a P-47 pilot from the 36th FS. It would be months before McGuire would erase the Japanese victory flag denoting this 'Val' kill from the side of his fighter, in spite of the victory having been officially awarded to the pilot of the Thunderbolt.

That mission on 26 December signalled the end of the 475th FG's scoring run during the first five months of its operational service. More than 275 Japanese aircraft had been claimed destroyed in air-to-air combat, with 25 pilots having lost their lives in return to all causes. Thus, the group had established an eleven-to-one victories-to-losses ratio, and achieved an outstanding average of 55 victories per month. Although this record would certainly not hold throughout the war, the group had already exceeded the expectations of its 'creator', Maj General Kenney.

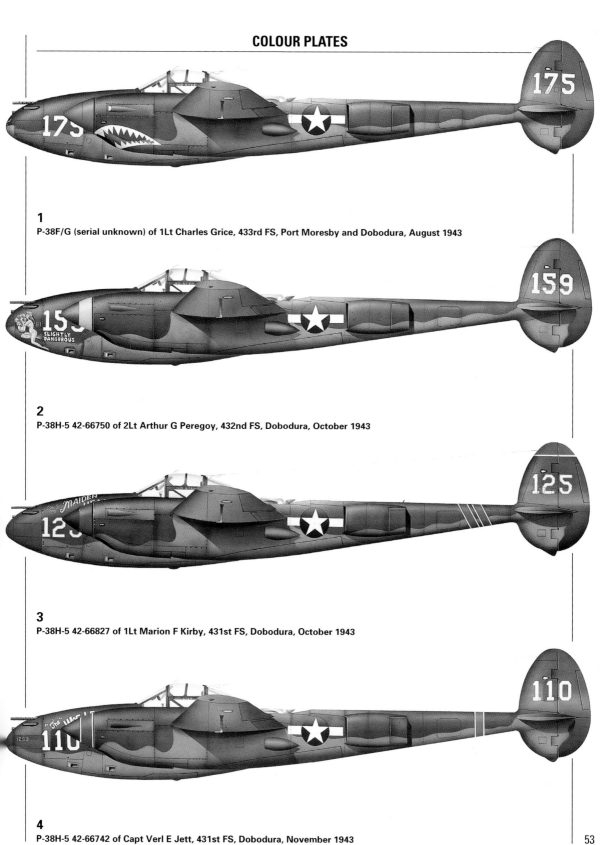

1
P-38F/G (serial unknown) of 1Lt Charles Grice, 433rd FS, Port Moresby and Dobodura, August 1943

2
P-38H-5 42-66750 of 2Lt Arthur G Peregoy, 432nd FS, Dobodura, October 1943

3
P-38H-5 42-66827 of 1Lt Marion F Kirby, 431st FS, Dobodura, October 1943

4
P-38H-5 42-66742 of Capt Verl E Jett, 431st FS, Dobodura, November 1943

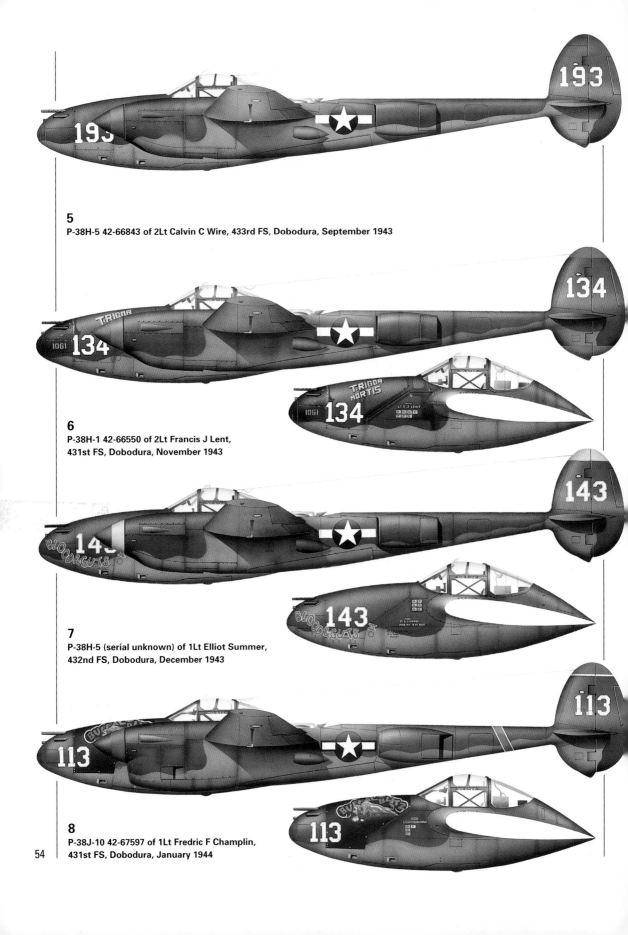

5
P-38H-5 42-66843 of 2Lt Calvin C Wire, 433rd FS, Dobodura, September 1943

6
P-38H-1 42-66550 of 2Lt Francis J Lent,
431st FS, Dobodura, November 1943

7
P-38H-5 (serial unknown) of 1Lt Elliot Summer,
432nd FS, Dobodura, December 1943

8
P-38J-10 42-67597 of 1Lt Fredric F Champlin,
431st FS, Dobodura, January 1944

9
P-38J-5 42-67290 of 1Lt Ferdinand E Hanson, 432nd FS, Dobodura, January 1944

10
P-38J-15 42-104035 of Maj Warren R Lewis, 433rd FS, Biak, June 1944

11
P-38H-1 42-66504 of 2Lt Perry J Dahl, 432nd FS, Dobodura, January 1944

12
P-38J-15 (serial unknown) of Maj Thomas B McGuire, 431st FS, Biak, late July 1944

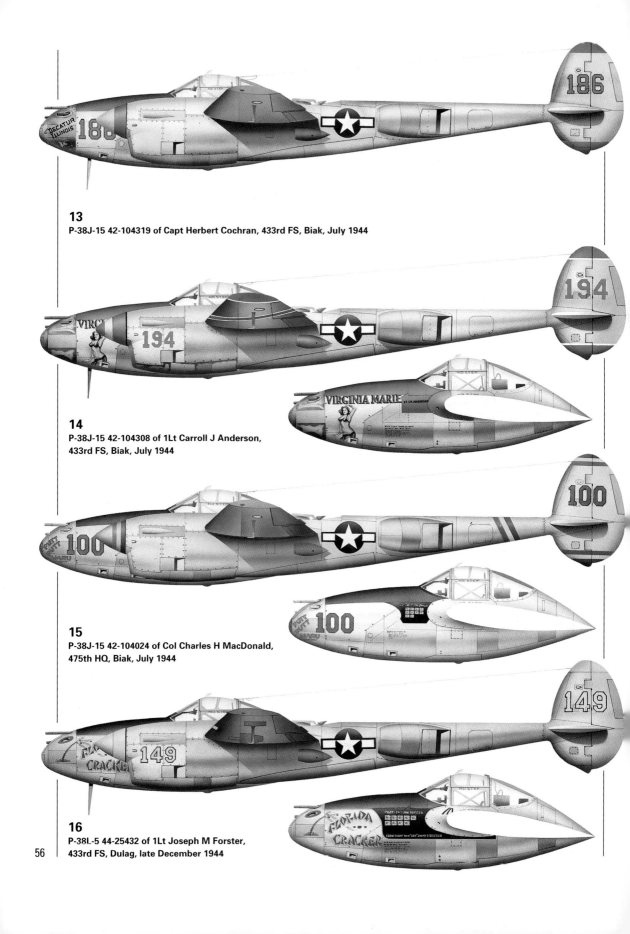

13
P-38J-15 42-104319 of Capt Herbert Cochran, 433rd FS, Biak, July 1944

14
P-38J-15 42-104308 of 1Lt Carroll J Anderson,
433rd FS, Biak, July 1944

15
P-38J-15 42-104024 of Col Charles H MacDonald,
475th HQ, Biak, July 1944

16
P-38L-5 44-25432 of 1Lt Joseph M Forster,
433rd FS, Dulag, late December 1944

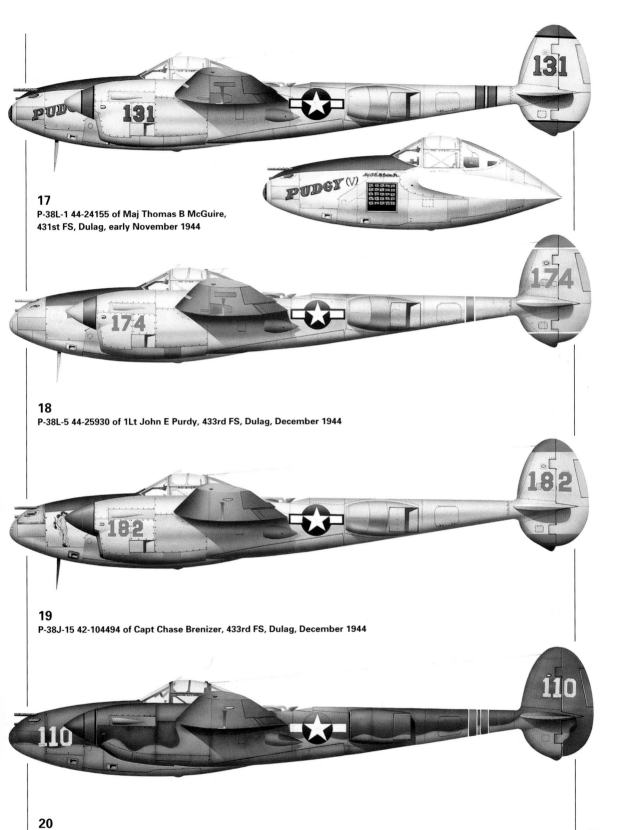

17
P-38L-1 44-24155 of Maj Thomas B McGuire,
431st FS, Dulag, early November 1944

18
P-38L-5 44-25930 of 1Lt John E Purdy, 433rd FS, Dulag, December 1944

19
P-38J-15 42-104494 of Capt Chase Brenizer, 433rd FS, Dulag, December 1944

20
P-38H-5 42-66836 of Maj Franklin A Nichols, 431st FS, Dobodura, October 1943

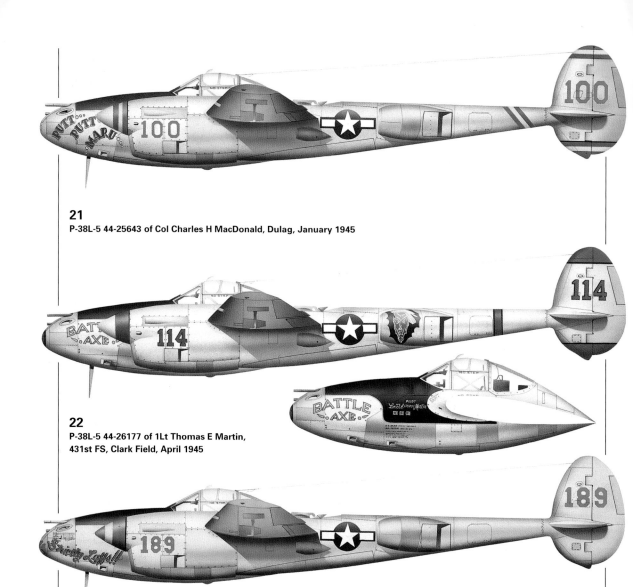

21
P-38L-5 44-25643 of Col Charles H MacDonald, Dulag, January 1945

22
P-38L-5 44-26177 of 1Lt Thomas E Martin,
431st FS, Clark Field, April 1945

23
P-38L-1 44-23987 of the 433rd FS, Clark Field, April 1945

24
P-38L-5 44-26404 of 1Lt Thomas F Fenton, 431st FS, Clark Field, April 1945

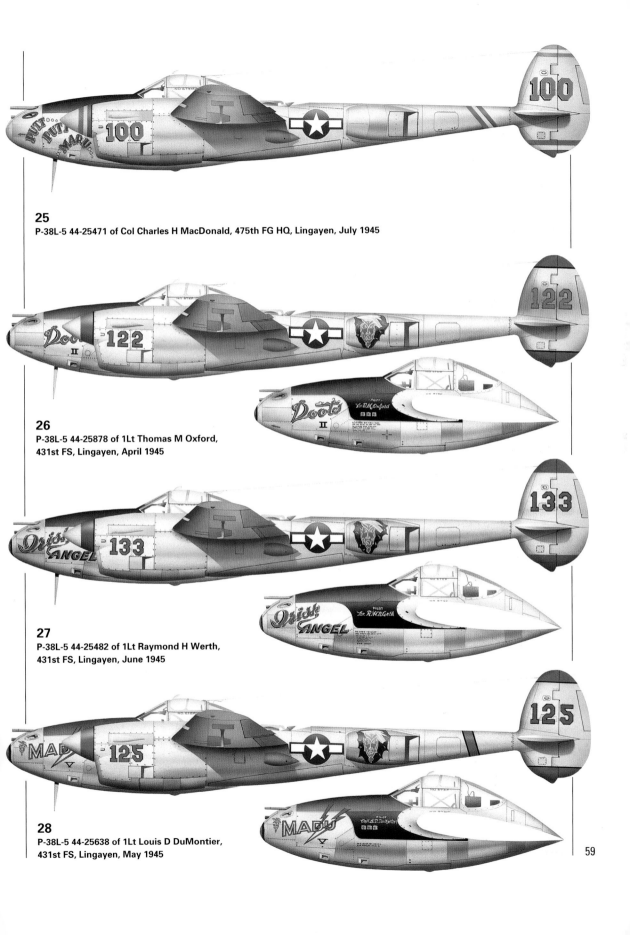

25
P-38L-5 44-25471 of Col Charles H MacDonald, 475th FG HQ, Lingayen, July 1945

26
P-38L-5 44-25878 of 1Lt Thomas M Oxford,
431st FS, Lingayen, April 1945

27
P-38L-5 44-25482 of 1Lt Raymond H Werth,
431st FS, Lingayen, June 1945

28
P-38L-5 44-25638 of 1Lt Louis D DuMontier,
431st FS, Lingayen, May 1945

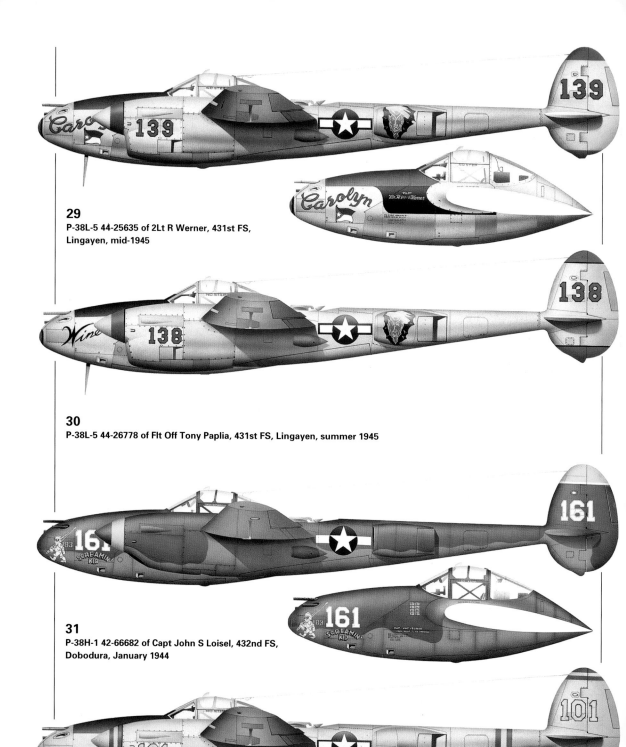

29
P-38L-5 44-25635 of 2Lt R Werner, 431st FS,
Lingayen, mid-1945

30
P-38L-5 44-26778 of Flt Off Tony Paplia, 431st FS, Lingayen, summer 1945

31
P-38H-1 42-66682 of Capt John S Loisel, 432nd FS,
Dobodura, January 1944

32
P-38L-5 44-25443 of Maj John S Loisel, 475th FG HQ, Dulag, January 1945

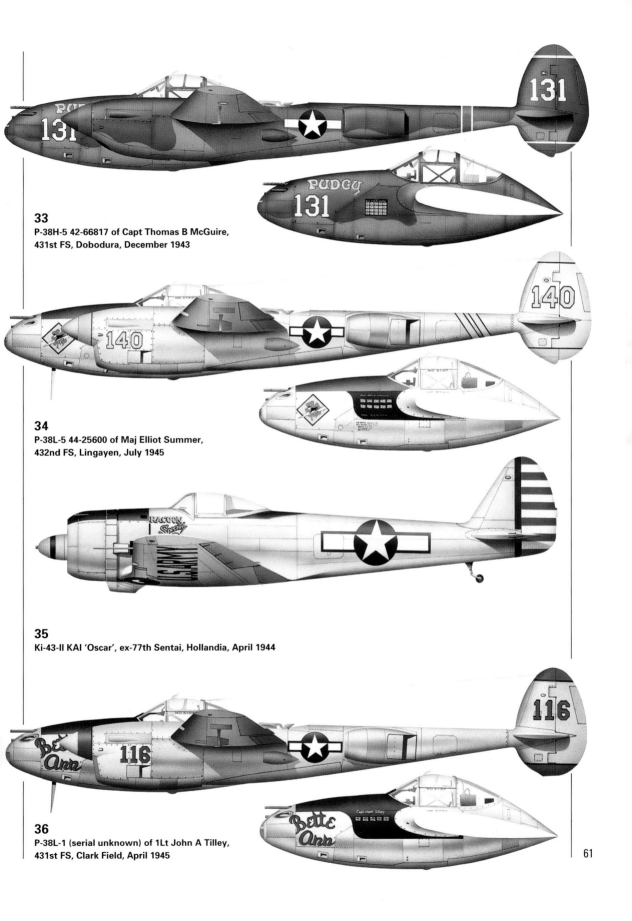

33
P-38H-5 42-66817 of Capt Thomas B McGuire,
431st FS, Dobodura, December 1943

34
P-38L-5 44-25600 of Maj Elliot Summer,
432nd FS, Lingayen, July 1945

35
Ki-43-II KAI 'Oscar', ex-77th Sentai, Hollandia, April 1944

36
P-38L-1 (serial unknown) of 1Lt John A Tilley,
431st FS, Clark Field, April 1945

1
475th Fighter Group

2
431st Fighter Squadron

3
432nd Fighter Squadron

4
433rd Fighter Squadron

LONG RANGE OVER WATER

January through to March 1944 saw the complete strangulation of Rabaul as an offensive base. Manus Island, in the Admiralties northwest of New Britain, was taken at the end of February to seal a ring around the Japanese base. Elsewhere, areas taken in the Solomon Islands were also consolidated at much the same time, and early the previous month the Saidor region just north of the Huon peninsula had fallen as Allied forces seized their first territory north of the Huon Gulf.

The 475th FG was heavily involved in the fighting during this period, with six pilots being killed in action. One of those lost was 1Lt William Ritter during a fighter sweep to Wewak on 18 January. Lt Col MacDonald led four squadrons of P-38s that day, which claimed 13 'Oscars' and 'Tonys' (including an 'Oscar' each to aces MacDonald, Jett and Gresham). Ritter, of the 432nd FS flew too close to the 'Tony' that he was shooting down and a piece of the disintegrating fighter flew back and tore off one of the P-38's wings. 2Lt John Michener, who was Ritter's wingman, saw the Lightning fall in flames without any sign of a parachute.

Ritter, who was an amiable and well-liked pilot, apparently managed to escape from his flaming aircraft, only to fall into the hands of a pitiless enemy. Word eventually reached the Allies that he had been summarily beheaded by his captors.

Attacks on Wewak continued throughout February and March in an effort to further reduce the base's potential to hinder Allied advances along the northern coast of New Guinea. The Wewak area would finally be invaded by Australian forces in May 1945, by which point the base was barely functioning.

1Lt William Ritter usually flew P-38J-15 '154', which is seen here serving as a backdrop for 432nd FS pilots in late 1943 – note the six Japanese flags beneath its cockpit. Ritter was reported missing during the 18 January 1944 fighter sweep of Wewak, and it was subsequently learned that he had been captured by the Japanese and summarily executed (*Author*)

Personnel from the 432nd FS's Ordnance Department pose for a group photograph in early 1944. They are, from left to right in the front row, Sgt George L Peters, unknown, Cpl K C Jones and Cpl Anthony L Pometto, Jnr. In the back row, again from left to right, are 1Lt Darrell W Morgan, Sgt Louis Necke, unknown, unknown and TSgt Charles E Bigelow (*Author*)

With Wewak effectively sidelined, the Fifth Air Force began supporting a new offensive against the former Dutch colonial capital of Hollandia, which represented the enemy's last viable defensive point south of the Vogelkop peninsula.

Allied aerial claims were admittedly exaggerated following the battles which took place over the town, with American pilots perhaps being the worst culprits. As claims were made in the heat of large scale combat, it is easy to see how honest mistakes were made. A decidedly unscientific survey estimates that as much as 40 per cent of all American claims could be discounted. Be that as it may, the JAAF had certainly been weakened by the time it was forced to consolidate its units around Hollandia.

On 16 January, for example, the newly deployed 'Oscars' and 'Tonys' of an inexperienced sentai reported losing ten fighters over the Saidor area to the P-40s of the highly-regarded 35th FS/8th FG. The Warhawk pilots in turn claimed 19 victories to set the high-scoring record for a single V Fighter Command squadron in an engagement in World War 2.

By the time of the assault on Hollandia there were fewer experienced Japanese pilots available to oppose Allied aircraft, and even those who were veterans now showed signs of trying to survive in combat, rather than taking on an ever more formidable enemy. Therefore, when American bombers finally appeared over the Hollandia area at the end of March, Japanese forces were already primed for defeat.

Only four squadrons of P-38s remained in V Fighter Command following the gruelling battles fought out over Rabaul and Wewak that finally ended in November 1943. In the weeks that followed, the 475th again incurred hostility from other fighter units in the Southwest Pacific when replacement P-38s newly arrived in-theatre were concentrated in

'Stuart Lawhead's Folly' was how the apparent wheels up landing of this 432nd FS P-38J-5 (42-67593) was described on the reverse of this photograph, taken in early 1944. This aircraft was duly repaired, only to be lost in a fatal crash on 11 June 1944 that killed 2Lt Troy Martin. The latter had been unable to retract his undercarriage upon taking off from Hollandia on a bomber escort mission, and whilst circling Lake Sentani as he attempted to jettison his external tanks, Martin experienced dual engine failure in 42-67593 and crashed into a swamp (*Author*)

the 80th FS/8th FG and the three squadrons of the 475th FG. Pilots assigned to the 49th FG's 9th FS were especially unhappy about giving up their Lightnings for the generally despised P-47, which the unit was forced to keep well into 1944.

As a point of fact, the 49th considered itself the seminal fighter group of the Southwest Pacific, and its crews resented the fact that the 475th had taken its 'lifeblood' in terms of skilled pilots, maintainers and replacement P-38s. Ex-49th FG CO Brig Gen Paul 'Squeeze' Wurtsmith, who was rapidly becoming a decisive force in Fifth Air Force operations in his capacity as Commander-in-Chief of V Fighter Command, and who considered his old unit with more than just a modicum of affection, stated publicly that he intended to give the 49th its head in P-38s and pilots when allocations were eventually increased.

Thus, leadership of future operations would probably go to the 49th FG, with lesser opportunities going to other groups such as the 475th. And this was indeed what transpired during the Philippines offensive, as the 49th was given territory to patrol in the promising Luzon area, while the 475th had to be content with leaner pickings in the Mindoro-Leyte-Negros triangle.

But all this lay in the future. The Hollandia threat had to first be neutralised, and the offensive began with four squadrons of P-38s available to the Fifth Air Force for bomber escort. The one Lightning squadron – the 80th – not controlled by the 475th in the campaign commenced escort operations when it took B-24s to their target as part of the initial attack mounted on Hollandia on 30 March 1944. All US aircraft returned from the successful raid, and 80th FS 'Headhunters' pilots claimed seven Japanese interceptors destroyed.

The following day it was the 431st FS that was given the job of escorting the 'heavies', 21 'Hades' squadron aircraft departing Nadzab airstrip No 3 at 0755 hrs and rendezvousing with B-24s 20 minutes later. Once all the Lightnings were correctly positioned above the bombers, the force headed for the target.

About 15 minutes before the formation reached Hollandia, the Lightnings were jumped by 15 Japanese fighters. 'Yellow Flight' was the last formation in the escort, and 1Lt Frank Monk ordered his pilots to drop their tanks when he saw enemy aircraft some 1000 ft above them, diving from the right towards the Lightnings in front of him. The 'Oscars' were heading for the tails of 'Green Flight', which was immediately in front of him, so Monk forced the Japanese pilots to turn away from their intended targets by breaking into them head on. One Ki-43 broke to the right, presenting Monk with the chance to rip away pieces of its canopy, engine and wing with a well-aimed burst of fire.

2Lt Horace 'Bo' Reeves was a new pilot in the squadron flying on Monk's wing throughout the mission, and he saw the Ki-43 burst into flames and disintegrate moments after it was hit.

2Lt Herman Zehring was leading 'Yellow Flight's' second element when he followed his leader into the fight. Looking around to clear his tail, Zehring saw his wingman, 2Lt Robert Donald, leaving the formation to chase after another 'Oscar'. He was later seen to join up with other P-38s in the area, and Zehring mentally promised him a tongue-lashing for leaving him in the middle of a dogfight when they got back to base. However, Donald ultimately paid a much higher price for breaking up section integrity, as he was subsequently listed as the only American loss for the day.

Later in the fight, 2Lt Zehring sighted 15 more enemy fighters attempting to attack the B-24s, and 1Lt Monk turned leadership of the flight over to him when he could not locate the 'Oscars' over Humboldt Bay. Zehring made the most of the opportunity and shot down two Ki-43s, one of which crashed on the shore of Humboldt Bay – these victories took his final tally to four kills.

1Lt 'Fran' Lent downed a pair of 'Oscars' (claimed as 'Zekes') to tally the last of his 11 victories, and other squadron pilots were credited with two more. One unconsummated attack was attributed to Capt Tom McGuire, who was beginning to feel the frustration of striving to become the leading US ace – he had not claimed a kill since 26 December 1943;

'I was leading "Green Flight". We made contact with the enemy 25 miles southeast of Hollandia at 1015 hrs. There were ten to fifteen "Oscars", "Zekes" and one "Tony". My flight was jumped from behind

*One of the first natural metal P-38J-15s to reach the 432nd FS undergoes maintenance at Nadzab just prior to the group's move to Biak (*Hoxie*)*

*Capt Tom McGuire is presented with yet another DFC by Brig Gen Wurtsmith at Hollandia in the spring of 1944. McGuire had received the DSC, three Silver Stars, five DFCs and 15 Air Medals by the time he was killed in action in January 1945. He was posthumously awarded the Medal of Honor in 1946 (*Author*)*

and above. "Yellow Flight" drove them off as I turned underneath and to the right to drive enemy aircraft off 1Lt Monk's flight ("Yellow Flight"). I got a short burst in, but the "Tony" half-rolled before I could do any damage. My second element snafued at that time.

'We stayed over the bombers and target area until 1110 hrs. The enemy pilots seemed non-aggressive, and appeared to be trying to escape after their first pass. A/A was very light. We covered the bombers back to 50 miles from Tadji, where we left them and proceeded home, landing at 1335 hrs.'

It was the 432nd FS's turn to shine when the weather improved enough for another strike to be made on Hollandia on 3 April. Some 17 P-38s (with the addition of Capt Richard I Bong, who tacked on to the unit on its approach to Hollandia in his V Fighter Command Lightning and went on to score his 25th victory in the ensuing engagement) guarded a mixed force of A-20s and B-25s that struck the target from 1135 hrs onwards.

Two pairs of 'Tony' fighters slipped behind the rear elements of 'Green Flight' and made separate attacks, 1Lt Clifford Mann, who had just gone into battle formation with Flt Off Joe Barton, spotting them at the very last minute. Mann ordered the flight to drop their external tanks, and watched in horror as two enemy fighters closed quickly on the inexperienced Barton. A violent roll and dive to the right lost the first two Ki-61s at 4000 ft, but the second pair of fighters then latched onto Barton's tail. Mann evaded again by diving steeply to the left, and he glanced back to see Barton rolling away in the same direction into a nearby bank of cloud. Subsequent visual sweeps and radio calls failed to find any trace of him, however, and Mann eventually had to head home when his fuel level became critical. Barton was the mission's only casualty.

Elsewhere, other flights were enjoying much better fortune. Capt John Loisel was leading 'Blue Flight' over the target when he heard calls from

This photograph of 1Lt 'Fran' Lent posing with his P-38H-1 42-66550 *T-RIGOR MORTIS* was taken in late October 1943. His score officially stood at seven at the time, but some enterprising soul scratched four more victory flags onto this print after Lent claimed his final kills in March 1944! (*Gregg*)

the A-20s that they were being attacked. He led his flight down to intercept a formation of eight 'Oscars', one of which fell to Loisel's guns. Future five-kill ace 1Lt Henry Condon, who was leading 'Green Flight', witnessed the first of Loisel's two victims crash into Sentani Lake just before he shot down his own Ki-43 on the south side of the lake.

The rest of 'Blue Flight' was also making its mark, with 1Lt Perry Dahl accounting for two more 'Oscars' (one claimed as a 'Zeke') to give him ace status. His wingman, 1Lt Joe Forster, gave the most impressive performance of the day, however, claiming two 'Tonys' and an 'Oscar' for his first confirmed victories. His afteraction report stated;

'The flight leader (Loisel) made an attack on the lead enemy fighter while I attacked the two-ship flight. My pass was to the front of the aircraft from the port side. The first enemy aeroplane – a "Tony" – was carrying aerial bombs. An explosion flashed immediately behind the engine, but I observed no further results. I continued my fire through the second "Tony", which was also carrying aerial bombs. It immediately burst into flames and crashed on a hillside. 1Lt Dahl observed this action. Pulling

Top and above
The 432nd FS's 1Lts Joe Forster (top) and Perry Dahl (above) were photographed in their P-38s during the Hollandia offensive in March-April 1944, when both aces claimed a number of their kills (*Author*)

back into string with my flight, I made several passes without effect. Following through, I made a head-on attack on an "Oscar". As it passed over, I saw smoke streaming from the engine. Banking into a turn, I saw another P-38 finish it off.

'After pulling back into string, I saw an "Oscar". I made several frontal and stern attacks and saw cannon flashes on his fuselage. I trailed him across Hollandia aerodrome and cornered him against a mountain. After a head-on pass, he began trailing smoke. Turning back, I closed in as the aeroplane began diving out of control. As the pilot got out on the wing I gave him a short burst. Both the pilot and his aeroplane continued in the dive and crashed. 2Lt Temple observed this aeroplane crashing into the mountain.'

Elsewhere on 3 April, 475th FS CO Lt Col Charles MacDonald was leading the escort at the head of 'Clover Red Flight' with his usual 432nd FS wingman, 1Lt John Hannan. Although MacDonald scored no kills on this mission, he did file an illuminating after action report;

'Approaching the southeast side of Sentani Lake, I observed six "Oscars" on the deck making for the A-20s. They were in loose string formation. We attacked and split them up. One "Oscar" got down over a swamp and kept turning and twisting as everyone made passes. 1Lt Summer ("White Flight" leader) shot him down. We attacked another "Oscar" who worked his way over Hollandia aerodrome before he was shot down by 1Lt Hannan. He crashed in the revetment area. I saw three crashed aeroplanes on the south side of the lake.

'Numerous small fires and dense smoke covered Hollandia airstrip. Light calibre A/A was intense. I observed a large ship in the harbour and numerous barges and luggers. The airstrips looked like junk yards.'

The 'Possum' flights of the 433rd FS duly added two more 'Oscars' to the 12 claimed by the 'Clover' flights. An additional ten claims were made by the 'Headhunters' of the 80th FS, and these victories combined virtually eradicated Hollandia's air defences. Granted, the actual losses suffered by the Japanese were certainly lower than those claimed by the P-38 pilots, but the decline in the enemy's aerial strength following this mission was marked nevertheless.

BLACK SUNDAY

Although 3 April saw the 475th FG claim its last victories over the Hollandia area, sadly the group would lose more pilots in the region in coming days. And these losses would be inflicted by the turbulent New Guinea weather rather than by the enemy, for the latter was now all but beaten. Proof of this came in intercepted messages sent by the Japanese garrison in Hollandia that urgently complained of dwindling supplies and an inability to counter Allied attacks.

Despite this intelligence, the Fifth Air Force was instructed to conduct one final air strike on Hollandia prior to the Allies launching an invasion on 22 April. A relatively large force of B-24s, B-25s and A-20s from seven bomb groups would be sent against targets in and around the town, with the bombers being protected by 70+ P-38s from the 475th and the 8th FGs – all three squadrons in the latter group had recently converted to the Lightning. These aircraft could have delivered a mighty blow had the weather cooperated.

The morning of 16 April dawned with gloomy and overcast skies that promised to have the mission scrubbed. The P-38 pilots were already planning to spend the day on the ground when sunshine eventually appeared to herald fine conditions to launch the mission. Just before noon, the Lightnings were sent aloft and rendezvoused with the bombers with little difficulty.

For the previous two days Allied weather services had been recommending that the mission be cancelled, but clear blue skies all the way to the target area seemed to prove the 'met men' wrong.

No interceptors were encountered over Hollandia, and the few anti-aircraft bursts that appeared soon after the bombers had made their devastating run on the target emphasised the poor condition of the Japanese defences below. It was an encouraging sign for the aircrews now returning home, and the P-38 pilots were especially ebullient thanks to the extra fuel they had in their tanks due to the absence of Japanese aerial opposition.

Rat-racing and dodging in and around the 'heavies', the fighter pilots frolicked to the delight of the bomber crews, who enjoyed the impromptu aerobatics show. Some distance away, however, ominous black clouds topping out above 30,000 ft were rapidly building up, and before long, the playful P-38 pilots would be sweating in terror as they desperately tried to find airstrips where they could land safely in an effort to escape the worst of the New Guinea weather.

Then the full scope of the deadly storm front was revealed to the American force when dark storm clouds descended from the north to trap them in a disappearing pocket of clear weather. When the horrifying truth dawned on them, the Lightning pilots tried to get radio fixes from nearby ground stations, while desperately attempting to follow the bombers which were already breaking up into individual flights so as to better rely on their own navigation equipment.

432nd FS pilot 2Lt Robert Hubner was heard by Capt Loisel making frantic calls for help, and although the veteran ace tried his best to calm his excited squadronmate down, the desperate radio calls eventually faded out and Hubner, and his element leader, 1Lt Jack Luddington, were never seen again. They were not the only Lightning pilots to be lost during this ill-fated mission.

The 433rd FS suffered the most grievously when five of its P-38s failed to return. 2Lts Louis Longman, Austin Neely and Lewis Yarbrough were simply lost somewhere in the murk, while 1Lts Bob Tomberg and Bud Wire had harrowing escapes.

The latter pilot was flying in company with new 433rd FS pilot 2Lt Mort Ryerson when they unsuccessfully attempted to join several bomber formations in the hope that they would guide them home. Having lost one group of B-25s when they broke up to make it through the weather individually, Wire then failed in his attempt to lead Ryerson above the storm. He then tried to find a clear path along the shore, following the coastline until he reached the Saidor area, where he tried to land at the tiny L-4 Piper Cub airstrip at Yamai.

Whilst manoeuvring his big fighter in high winds for an approach over the sea, Wire mushed his Lightning into a wave and was lucky to emerge from his sinking P-38 without serious injury. He bobbed about in his

TSgt Shive and 2Lt Bob Tomberg pose for the camera in November 1943. Five months later, Tomberg would make an amazing trek after he was forced down in the New Guinea jungle by a deadly storm front (*Tomberg via Cook*)

flotation gear until a small boat picked him up. Ryerson was fortunate enough to make it all the way back home.

Having been in-theatre since 1942, 1Lt Robert Tomberg of the 433rd FS knew just how treacherous New Guinea weather could be, so he took to his parachute and was lucky enough to land in a clearing near thick forest. Although suffering minor injuries on landing, he was able to walk to an airfield in the Saidor area, where he hitched a ride back to Finschhafen in the gunner's position of an A-20.

Tomberg's squadronmates 2Lts Joe Price and Stanley Northrup managed to crash-land at Saidor, where their P-38s were handed over to service squadrons for repairs while they returned to duty with minor injuries.

2Lt Milton MacDonald of the 431st FS was less fortunate, however, and the wreckage of his Lightning was eventually discovered near Efu village. The young pilot's remains were not reclaimed until after the war, however.

Ten P-38s from the 475th FG crashed, killing six pilots, during the most devastating day the Fifth Air Force would ever endure. Overall, 54 aircrew and 46 aircraft were lost.

SECURING NEW GUINEA

Between 22 April and the beginning of June, enemy forces along the previously impregnable northern coast of New Guinea were swept aside by the Allies. The 4th Japanese Air Army was all but wiped out during this period, with its bases being seized and surviving aircraft shot down as they attempted to escape to the northwest Vogelkop peninsula.

The Fifth Air Force was combined with the Thirteenth Air Force during this campaign to form the Far East Air Forces (FEAF), which would in turn be responsible for supporting campaigns in the Philippines, Central Pacific, Borneo and the former Dutch East Indies.

Despite these significant organisational changes, within V Fighter Command the great 'ace race' continued unabated. Indeed, on 12 April Maj Dick Bong had broken the long-standing World War 1 record of Capt Eddie Rickenbacker when he had taken his tally to 28 kills following the destruction of three Ki-43s over Hollandia.

Capt Tom McGuire was Bong's closest living rival (22-victory ace Col Neel Kearby had been killed in action on 5 March 1944), but as

433rd FS CO Maj Warren Lewis claimed his seventh, and last, confirmed victory on 19 May 1944 when he downed an F1M 'Pete' reconnaissance biplane off Noemfoor Island. He claimed an 'Oscar' damaged in the Jefman-Samate area the following month. Lewis turned command of 'Possum Squadron' over to Capt Campbell Wilson in August 1944 (*Author*)

mentioned earlier, he was enduring a barren run that had started, following his 16 kills, on 26 December 1943. He had still not added to his tally by the time Bong was sent home on leave in mid April. However, in May and June McGuire claimed four victories to take his tally to 20 kills.

McGuire and his fellow pilots in the 475th FG would get more opportunities to add to their scores in June, when reports from Allied reconnaissance aircraft and submarines suggested that a strong Japanese naval force was lurking off the coast of Biak island, northwest of New Guinea. The enemy were resisting Allied invasion attempts with remarkable vehemence, fighting hard to retain control of its strategically important airfields. Several sweeps were made by the 475th FG of the waters north of the island but no Japanese vessels were located.

An enemy troop convoy did indeed exist, however, the naval vessels carrying 2500 troops sent from the Philippines to reinforce Biak.

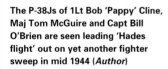

The P-38Js of 1Lt Bob 'Pappy' Cline, Maj Tom McGuire and Capt Bill O'Brien are seen leading 'Hades flight' out on yet another fighter sweep in mid 1944 (*Author*)

Ducking in and out of weather fronts, the reinforcement force dodged back and forth with little hope of breaking through the waves of Allied aircraft searching for it.

On 7 June Col MacDonald led an escort force of 432nd FS P-38s that were covering B-25s sent to find and attack the Japanese convoy. However, the mission fell foul of poor weather and the Lightnings landed on Wakde Island instead. The next day the enemy vessels made a determined bid to reach Biak in better weather across open seas, and this allowed ten B-25s, covered by 17 P-38s from the 432nd and 433rd FSs (again led by MacDonald), to intercept the ships near Manokwari Island.

Col MacDonald claimed his 11th kill during the engagement which ensued, and details of this victory were outlined in his after action report;

'We approached at the same level as the B-25s and then climbed to the right in order to divert anti-aircraft fire away from them as they turned to the left to begin their bombing runs. At the same time we sighted enemy aircraft about 3000 ft above us, so we started climbing towards them. Three more enemy aircraft then came from behind the clouds and passed about 1000 ft above us. We waited for them to make a move, but they did not seem anxious to engage us. Then we sighted four "Zekes" and started after them from "nine o'clock".

'The leader turned into me as though to make a head-on pass, but he seemed afraid to try it. I got a 30-degree head-on shot, led him two radii, and then fired a two-second burst. As I looked back I saw that he had burst into flame around the engine. Capt Zach Dean saw him crash into the water. This action took place at 5000 ft directly over the destroyers, where the "Zekes" apparently thought we wouldn't follow them.

'When we entered that area the enemy formation broke up and ran. I followed what I think was an "Oscar". As I was overtaking him, he dived through an overcast at 3000 ft. I followed, fired a short burst and saw him start smoking. I could also see where part of his wing peeled back from a

Maj Arsenio R 'Sam' Fernandez replaced the redoubtable Maj LeRoy Richardson as group adjutant. Tragically, the popular Richardson went missing when his transport aircraft crashed during a routine flight in September 1944. Fernandez was rotated home at around the same time (*Hoxie*)

Below and bottom
The Allies found various wrecked
Japanese aircraft littering the
Hollandia airstrips when they
occupied them in mid May 1944 –
the aircraft in the top photograph are
Ki-51s and the fighter in the bottom
shot is a Ki-43. Indeed, the invasion
had progressed so swiftly that
numerous crates full of aircraft parts
were found still unpacked. Surviving
Japanese personnel in the area were
forced to evacuate towards the
north, taking with them only what
they could carry (*Hanks and Krane*)

cannon shot. He pulled back into the overcast and I followed him in, but losing sight of him in the soup, I dived out. Then I saw him again, and as I closed in, he flew into a large cumulus cloud. I went right in behind him, and as we came out the other side, I got another burst at him. He did a quick 180-degree turn and again headed back into the cloud. I fired another shot at that time, and as the enemy aircraft entered the cloud I followed him, still shooting. I then saw a bright orange flash in the mist, and when I came out the other side of the cloud I could no longer see the Nip aircraft.'

A steady build up of cloud cover over the convoy made the confirmation of several certain victories impossible to achieve, although 1Lt Perry Dahl managed to confirm one 'Oscar' destroyed and another probably destroyed, while 1Lt Clifford Mann also destroyed a Ki-43. Dahl subsequently lived up to his nickname 'Lucky' when his landing gear failed and he simply walked away from what should have been a serious crash when his fighter speared into

trees and was totally destroyed.

Luck was not entirely with the bombers, however, for three of their number were shot down over the target ships and the remaining seven were all badly shot up. One vessel was sunk and three others badly damaged, and this was enough to discourage the Japanese convoy from trying to reach Biak.

Eight days days later, on 16 June, recently promoted Maj Tom McGuire claimed two victories when he led the 431st FS on a B-25 escort to Jefman

1Lt Bill Gronemeyer of the 431st FS departs Owi Island in his newly-repaired P-38J-15 42-104021 *Little GRACE II* on 19 June 1944 (*Author*)

Island. The squadron initially flew from Hollandia to Wakde Island to refuel, where Col MacDonald experienced electrical problems in his P-38 that forced him to relinquish the role of mission leader over to a delighted McGuire. Having refuelled, the P-38s took off again at 0930 hrs and rendezvoused with the bombers over Roon Island at 1140 hrs. Within 90 minutes they had intercepted Ki-43s and a solitary Ki-51 'Sonia' tactical reconnaissance aircraft.

To the astonishment of his squadronmates, McGuire actually manoeuvred with the 'Oscars', following one of the agile Japanese fighters into a reverse turn and claiming it destroyed after it blew up under the weight of his fire. With a 'Sonia' also shot down during this engagement, McGuire's score now stood at 22.

Other 'Hades' pilots added an additional six 'Oscars' to the mission tally, including two for Capt Paul Morriss to take his final tally to five kills.

This close up view of 1Lt Bill Gronemeyer's *Little GRACE II* reveals five victory flags beneath the fighter's cockpit. Gronemeyer was an exuberant 431st FS pilot who was officially credited with four victories by the time he left the 475th FG. He was subsequently killed in a routine training flight in the USA (*Author*)

1Lt Frank Monk also scored his fifth, and final, kill, while 2Lt 'Bo' Reeves claimed the first of his eventual six victories. Capt Bill Gronemeyer downed the third of his four victories, and McGuire's wingman, 2Lt Enrique Provencio, claimed his first of two kills.

LINDBERGH VISIT

Col MacDonald had just finished a refreshing dip in the cold stream behind his quarters on Hollandia and was settling down for a game of checkers with his executive officer, newly-promoted Lt Col Meryl Smith, when a tall civilian came up to introduce himself. MacDonald was so involved with his game that he initially paid little attention to the presence of this mildly irritating stranger. When the man began asking them intelligent and very technical questions, both MacDonald and Smith looked up and recognised the eminent aviator Charles Augustus Lindbergh.

During his time in the Pacific, Lindbergh put his infamous anti-war sentiments behind him by offering technical advice that brought amazing performance from US combat aircraft in-theatre. V Fighter Command benefitted greatly from his expertise in long distance flying, Lindbergh's

Lt Col Meryl Smith, Charles Lindbergh and Col Charles MacDonald pose for an informal photograph in July 1944 (*Gregg*)

suggestions allowing its pilots to extend the range of their existing P-38 and P-47 fighters to such a degree that they could confidently operate over the unbelievable distances that their command now had to contend with.

Lindbergh spent time with virtually every P-38 and P-47 squadron in-theatre between May and late August 1944, passing on some extremely useful tips and techniques that increased their fighters' endurance. He explained how it was possible for Lightnings, for example, to fly mission distances in excess of 800 miles which tested the limits of the pilot more than the machine itself. Lindbergh quickly became a legend once again to men who had been little more than idolising boys when he spanned the Atlantic in May 1927.

Although revered in the frontline, it must be said that Lindbergh was less than completely taken with the 475th FG during his stay with the group. He certainly came to admire the skill and bravery of individual pilots and commanders, but his sensibilities were offended by some of the group's practices. One of the things that caused him the most concern was the 475th's general attitude towards the enemy. Lindbergh felt that most of the personnel in the group acted like pirates rather than professional

Charles Lindbergh pre-flights a P-38J at Biak prior to taking off on an operational flight in early August 1944. Note the tail of Maj McGuire's *PUDGY III* in the background (*Author*)

Like most USAAF fighter and bomber units in World War 2, the 475th FG applied risqué nose art to most of its aircraft. Artwork such as this seen here offended Lindbergh to the point where he thought that the group's pilots were little more than flying buccaneers! (*Hoxie, Bates and Krane*)

soldiers when dealing with the enemy. Indeed, even the Japanese at Rabaul became aware of the 'Satan's Angels', as the aviators in the 475th were called, and 'Radio Tokyo' nicknamed the group the 'Bloody Butchers'.

Many pilots thought it part of the rules of the game to gang up on damaged Japanese aircraft as they tried to reach the safety of home. Lightning pilots also routinely strafed their enemy counterparts as they dangled helplessly in their parachutes. Several downed Japanese pilots bobbing in Rabaul's Simpson Harbour also had to dive for safety when marauding P-38s sporting distinctive red, yellow or blue tails threatened to strafe them. Considering the

generally pitiless regard that the Japanese had for their prisoners of war in the Pacific, Lindbergh's criticism seems unusually harsh.

Lindbergh also objected to the unusually graphic artwork that adorned many of the group's P-38s. Drawings of unclad women and barbarous maledictions against their opponents were the usual subjects of this artwork, which was carried on both sides of the aircraft's nose. In general, the 475th crews shrugged when they were made aware of Lindbergh's complaints, and took it as something of a compliment that they were rough on the enemy.

Lindbergh's first flight with the 475th came on 27 June 1944, just 24 hours after meeting Col MacDonald and Lt Col Smith. The latter pilots accompanied Maj McGuire and Lindbergh on a reconnaissance mission to Jefman and Samate Islands, where they managed to inflict some damage on a pair of Japanese barges during a series of strafing passes.

The second mission that Lindbergh flew with the 475th was another reconnaissance to Nabire and Sagan, situated along the coastline of Geelvink Bay, in northwestern New Guinea. When Lindbergh landed

Maj McGuire's then new P-38L-1 *"Pudgy IV"* is seen on Biak in late September. The aircraft was adorned with 22 Japanese victory flags beneath its cockpit at the time (*Crow*)

1Lt Robert Crosswait of the 431st FS was posted missing in action in P-38J-10 42-67793 following one of the 475th FG's first dive-bombing missions to Noemfoor Island on 30 June 1944 (*Author*)

431st FS P-38J-15 *Doris* served
with the unit during the Hollandia
offensive in March/April 1944
(*Author*)

and his P-38 was checked out, the groundcrew was amazed to find that he had considerably more fuel left in the tanks of his fighter than the other members of his flight. Lindbergh noted the reason for the low fuel consumption in his postwar book, *Wartime Journals of Charles Lindbergh*;

'I landed on the Hollandia strip at 1708 hrs after a six-hour-and-fifty-minute flight. All during the day I had been holding my engine down to get a check on minimum fuel consumption. Landed with 210 gallons in my tanks.'

Any reservations held by group pilots about how the ideas of this aviation pioneer could benefit a modern combat organisation disappeared in the face of actual practice over coming days. It soon became common for pilots to get pointers from Lindbergh on the art of reducing manifold pressure during combat flights in order to reduce fuel consumption by almost half. The 475th FG's already hard-worked groundcrews were less than enthusiastic, however, when they realised that the methods suggested by Lindbergh would inevitably foul their fighters' Allison V1710 engines, thus both hastening and complicating servicing.

Some pilots who flew long missions with Lindbergh became excited when the usual halfway point was reached for a P-38 mission and he would calmly order engine settings for an extended flight. Inexperienced

Maj McGuire and Charles Lindbergh
are seen deep in conversation
following a long range sweep from
Biak in late July 1944 (*Author*)

LONG RANGE OVER WATER

Lightning pilots would then sit in cold dread of an engine sputtering into
lifelessness until the flight would land as much as eight hours after
take-off. A grinning Lindbergh would jump up on the wing of the newly
initiated pilot to declare, 'See, didn't I tell you we could do it?'

For most of his time with the 475th, Lindbergh was under the care of
Maj Tom McGuire, much to the consternation of some of the pilots in the
431st FS. McGuire would routinely treat Lindbergh with apparent
disdain, ordering him to do menial tasks or speaking to him as an
underling. Lindbergh, knowing that he was a guest under already
trying conditions in a combat zone, had little recourse for any slight that
he received.

However, other veterans remember that the interplay between
McGuire and Lindbergh was on the light side, with the venerable
practical joker Lindbergh giving as good as he got. One pilot recalled
McGuire ordering Lindbergh to fetch his beloved battered service hat,
and Lindbergh returning with a flight cap that was far too big for him, and
which was adorned with the single gold bar of a second lieutenant!

Lindbergh was right in being discreet about the fact that he flew combat
missions. He even furtively claimed to have destroyed a Ki-51 'Sonia' of
the 73rd Independent Chutai over the island of Ceram, off the west coast

of the Vogelkop peninsula, on 28 July. MacDonald was leading a formation of 433rd FS aircraft, one of which was flown by Lindbergh, at the time, so the eventual fall out when the incident was revealed to Fifth Air Force HQ came down heavily on him. Being a civilian, Lindbergh was forbidden from partaking in combat missions, even though tacit approval for the flight had been tendered. MacDonald was duly sent home on leave as punishment.

Aside from the embarrassment caused to V Fighter Command by this incident, Lindbergh's range development work with the 475th FG had also raised further problems for the command when it was publicly revealed that it had been telling V Bomber Command for weeks that it could not facilitate their requests for long range fighter escorts! In reality, the Lightning groups had been flying freelance sweeps in search of enemy aircraft, as Lindbergh's kill had shown.

Col MacDonald shrugged off being made the scapegoat for the failings of senior officers in V Fighter Command, instead making the most of his enforced leave by seeing his new born son. He would return to the group in October, but just prior to his departure for the USA, he managed to fly one more long distance mission to Palau Island on 1 August and claim an A6M2N 'Rufe' floatplane fighter and a 'Val' dive-bomber to take his tally to 13 kills.

Lindbergh left the 475th FG in mid August and continued to offer advice to several other units prior to being taken out of the theatre later in the month. He had done yeoman service for the Allied cause in the Pacific, even though he stated that he would not accept a commission whilst President Franklin D Roosevelt was in the White House. Roosevelt, in

Brig Gen Paul 'Squeeze' Wurtsmith, Col Charles MacDonald and Brig Gen Freddie Smith pose on Biak in front of MacDonald's P-38J-15 42-104024, which was written off in early August 1944 (Cooper)

Capt William O'Brien of the 431st FS was killed on 4 August 1944 when the Ki-61 he was attacking looped up and crashed head-on into his P-38J-15 42-104161. The 'Tony' was credited to him as his fourth victory (Author)

C-47s line up at Hollandia in mid July 1944, ready to transport the 475th FG's air echelon to Biak. Heavy equipment was shipped by sea aboard several US Navy LSTs, whilst ground echelons took whatever transport was assigned them (*Hanks*)

turn, is quoted as saying that he would never offer one to Lindbergh in any case! The great aviation pioneer had done as much as anyone could as a civilian to aid the Allied cause in the Pacific, and the results were immediately obvious in the ever-widening scope of 475th FG operations.

BALIKPAPAN

In mid June 1944, the group moved to Biak Island, near Geelvink Bay, in the Vogelkop peninsula. Although battles were still raging nearby to ensure the security of this strategically-positioned island, V Fighter Command felt that it was worth the risk basing one of its most prized units close to the enemy. Thanks to its location so far west, and with Lindbergh's advice on fuel monitoring being rigorously adhered to, the 475th, with careful staging through other 'bare base' airstrips in the region, could now escort heavy bombers sent to strike targets as far away as Mindanao or Borneo.

These missions would allow the Allies to knock out the all-important oil production facilities at Balikpapan, in the former Dutch East Indies, which the Japanese had been so anxious to seize in 1941. Oil was the life blood of the enemy's war effort, and virtually all of Japan's supplies came from refineries in this area.

The first escorted mission to Balikpapan was mounted on 10 October 1944, and the Lightnings involved staged through recently captured bases on Morotai Island. It was a generally successful operation, with P-47 pilots claiming 12 Japanese fighters destroyed and their P-38 counterparts six. Envious pilots from other groups, including the 475th, would get their chance to tangle with enemy fighters over Balikpapan just four days later.

On 14 October Lightnings from the 9th FS/49th FG would cover Fifth Air Force B-24s, as would 13 P-38s from the 432nd FS, led by deputy group CO, Lt Col Meryl Smith. Flying a P-38L-1, he took off from Biak with 'Clover Red Flight' at 0645 hrs and flew through clear weather until the Lightning pilots reached the target area four hours later. As Smith neared Balikpapan, he could hear that the P-38s of the 9th FS were busy

Capt Billy Gresham was a highly regarded pilot in the 432nd FS, having claimed six victories between September 1943 and March 1944. On 2 October 1944, he departed Biak alone in newly-delivered P-38L-1 44-23958 (fitted with aileron boost and compressibility flaps), having planned to air test the fighter. Gresham failed to return, and the wreckage of his Lightning was found the next day northwest of Borokoe airstrip, with his body nearby, wrapped in a partly deployed parachute (*Hoxie*)

tangling with a large force of enemy fighters through the pilots' excited radio chatter.

Six A6M3 'Hamps' were soon spotted above the milky white clouds, and Smith interposed his fighters between them and the bombers so as to prevent the latter from being attacked. The enemy pilots were skilled enough to dodge in and out of the clouds, thus stopping the 'Clover' pilots from successfully engaging them, but also ruining any chance they had of repelling the bombers.

Smith made several passes at individual interceptors before he at last got a good burst in at one of the 'Hamps'. His flight leaders were behind him, and they saw the enemy fighter burst into flames and fall away for Smith's seventh kill. 1Lt Joe Forster also successfully engaged a 'Zeke', thus bringing up his fourth victory.

The kills claimed by the 475th FG's leading scorer on this mission were not added to the group's overall total, however. When Maj Tom McGuire discovered that the 431st FS were not involved in this operation, he had somehow managed to get himself onto the mission roster of his former unit, the 9th FS/29th FG, as wingman for 11-kill ace Maj Jerry Johnson!

Johnson and McGuire had duly led their force of 17 P-38s into a group of about 25 Japanese interceptors that were trying to reach the B-24s. Both men sparred with the enemy fighters until McGuire got in behind an 'Oscar' that had been damaged by Johnson before excess speed had made the latter overshoot the target. Anxious not to make the same mistake, McGuire throttled back and set the Ki-43 ablaze, convincing the Japanese pilot to bail out. In turn, Johnson shot down a second 'Oscar' and a Ki-44 'Tojo', and McGuire also claimed a 'Tojo' after chasing the fighter in a dive through cloud down to about 1500 ft above the water, where the Japanese aircraft burst into flames and crashed. Minutes later he destroyed a third fighter that he identified as a 'Hamp', the A6M3 bursting into flames and going down, as witnessed by Johnson.

Unknown to McGuire, his fruitful, but furtive, mission with the rival 49th FG was being monitored by Col MacDonald, who had arrived back in-theatre that very day and resumed command of the group from Lt Col Smith. McGuire had left for the 9th FS camp elsewhere on Biak on the evening of 13 October, so he was unaware of MacDonald's return until he himself came back to the 475th on the 15th. Veterans swear that McGuire virtually rolled out of MacDonald's office after the wrathful commander had finished admonishing him, but MacDonald himself always gallantly denied any memory of dealing with his squadron commander (McGuire had become CO of the 431st FS on 2 May 1944), who had added three kills to the scoreboard of an arch rival fighter group.

McGuire's problems were minor in comparison to those of Capt Joe Forster, who had an engine shot out in his successful bid for a fourth

This close-up of Maj McGuire's immaculate *"Pudgy IV"* reveals its pilot's scoreboard as of early October 1944. His next three victories were claimed on the 14 October mission to Balikpapan, when he was at the controls of a P-38 from the 49th FG (*Author*)

aerial victory. The future ace subsequently set a record for single-engined flight in a P-38 when he covered the 850 miles back to the nearest friendly landing strip.

1Lt Ferdinand Hanson remembered the mission some 50 years later with an understandably hazy command of details, but an interesting and lighthearted view of the dangers involved;

'We landed at Halmahera fighter strip on our way back and started to count noses. "Where is Joe Forster – he's late?" Word was out that he was on a single engine, having been shot up and leaking coolant. As I recall, most of us quickly fuelled up and flew back to Biak. Joe was a good pilot, and we knew he'd make it. There was no use in missing our whisky ration just for him, and the sack would feel good after such a long flight.

'Well, Joe made it back and landed in the evening twilight at Biak. He later asked "Why didn't you guys wait for me? I could have been shot down, my only engine was overheating, I could have crashed at sea, I might have run out of gas – geeze – it was getting dark!" We simply shrugged our shoulders, went and got some G.I. soap and headed for the beach, intent on discovering how good the fishing was!'

1Lt Joe Forster strikes a valiant pose soon after surviving his epic 800-mile single-engined flight between Balikpapan and New Guinea (*Hoxie*)

THE PHILIPPINES

Following the long range strike on Balikpapan on 14 October 1944, and the successful commencement of the campaign to retake the Philippines six days later, the 475th FG began moving from Biak to Dulag, on the island of Leyte, on the 28th of that month. The initial invasion of Leyte had taken the Japanese completely by surprise, and the naval battle of Leyte Gulf which raged from 23 to 26 October virtually eliminated the IJN threat following the sinking of four fleet carriers and most other major warships of the Japanese fleet. Fully aware of how quickly the campaign was progressing, and anxious to see action, the 475th FG had to wait until 1 November to take on the enemy over the Philippines.

In the vanguard of the action was Maj Tom McGuire, who, earlier that same day, had led 17 'Hades' pilots in a ferry flight with elements of the 49th FG to the newly-won Tacloban airstrip. His unit had departed Morotai Island, in the Dutch East Indies, at 0730 hrs and arrived overhead Tacloban three hours later.

Upon making radio contact with a fighter controller at the base, McGuire was asked if he and his squadronmates had sufficient fuel remaining to patrol over the airfield, as Leyte was on red alert at the time. He readily agreed to help out, and his after action report reveals details of the first of 14 kills that the 475th FG's ranking ace would claim over the Philippines in two months of near constant action;

The fearsome sign and scoreboard that greeted visitors to the 431st FS's briefing tent at Dulag, on Leyte, during the campaign in the Philippines (*Author*)

The 432nd FS chose to have just one sign that combined both its name and its scoreboard (*Author*)

Maj Tom McGuire's P-38L-1 44-24155 *PUDGY (V)* was photographed perfectly illuminated at Tacloban immediately after its pilot had downed a 'Tojo' to register his 25th confirmed kill on 1 November 1944. This aircraft proved to be McGuire's most successful fighter, with the ace claiming 14 victories in it between 1 November and 26 December (*Author*)

'I took up patrol ten miles southwest of Tacloban at 10,000 ft with two flights, sending "Blue" and "Green Flights" up to 15,000 ft. At 1115 hrs we sighted one probable "Tojo" about 1000 ft above us. The enemy aircraft turned south and started a shallow dive for cloud cover. I gave chase, catching him just south of San Pablo. I fired one burst at 45 degrees deflection from 300 yards, getting hits and observing an explosion around the cockpit. I closed up to 50 ft, firing another two bursts. The "Tojo's" tail came apart and he started straight down, spinning and crashing into the hills. Flt Off Edward J O'Neil witnessed this action. We resumed patrol for a short while, after which we landed at Tacloban at 1200 hrs.'

This action signalled the beginning of a momentous two months of combat for the pilots of the 475th FG. When the JAAF and IJN recovered sufficiently from the shock of invasion and the decisive defeat of the Imperial Fleet, they responded by attacking Allied forces in the Philippines with every airworthy aircraft that they possessed, hoping to check the invasion.

From the end of October 1944 until early January 1945, many aerial victories were scored, especially by the pilots of the 49th and 475th FGs. However, these engagments would be the last great air battles fought in

The 433rd FS also had a HQ sign, which featured the unit's original emblem. The latter was inexplicably changed immediately postwar (*Author*)

432nd FS pilot 2Lt Calvin O Anderson usually flew as Col MacDonald's wingman whenever the latter sortied with the 'Clover Squadron' in the final months of 1944. When the colonel was not flying, Anderson got to lead his own section, and on 12 November he downed both an 'Oscar' and a 'Hamp' over Leyte (*Hoxie*)

the Southwest Pacific, and they would ultimately cost the 475th the life of its foremost fighter ace.

The group first's large-scale clash with the JAAF over the Philippines occurred during the morning of 10 November, and the clash almost saw the 432nd FS's 1Lt Perry Dahl (in P-38L 44-23957) lose his life. Dahl was the pride of his hometown on Mercer Island, Washington state, having claimed six Japanese aircraft shot down in seven months of combat. Nicknamed 'Lucky', he had negotiated every hazard of aerial combat with a buoyant spirit, which he would need in abundance on this particular operation, which almost proved to be his last.

Col MacDonald was once again leading the 432nd FS on this date, the unit having been scrambled to attack aircraft detected approaching Ormoc Bay. Twelve P-38s encountered a flight of four Japanese fighters, and MacDonald chased an 'Oscar' in and out of the clouds until he caught the Ki-43 with a concentrated burst of fire that set the aeroplane burning. MacDonald's wingman, 2Lt Calvin Anderson, subsequently reported witnessing the enemy pilot bail out.

MacDonald then noticed that his Lightning was inexplicably running low on fuel, so he turned the leadership of the squadron over to Dahl and hastily returned to Tacloban with Anderson. Dahl continued patrolling the area with his nine charges, and eventually he chased a lone Zero into a nearby bank of cloud. His initial frustration at having lost a certain kill gave way to elation when 16 enemy fighters were sighted flying serenely through the broken, dark, undercast. Dahl had his P-38s stalk the enemy aircraft until they broke out of the cloud cover into clear air, whereupon they were quickly identified as 'Tony' fighters.

Making sure that his squadron-mates carried plenty of airspeed into the engagement, Dahl dived on the Ki-61s from some 500 ft above the hapless JAAF fighters. He singled out the leading 'Tony' and fired a burst at it with about 45 degrees of deflection. Dahl watched the bullets hit the engine cowling and cockpit, then saw the Ki-61 fall away out of control, trailing smoke all the way down until it hit the water northwest of Ponson Island. No fewer than ten other 'Tonys' followed this aircraft down, with 2Lts Henry Toll and Richard Kiick both claiming two Ki-61s apiece.

2Lt Henry Toll was cited as the designer of the 432nd FS's emblem. He was also a skilled fighter pilot, claiming three victories over the Philippines (*Author*)

Dahl's after action report describes with laconic detail the harrowing events he then had to endure after claiming his seventh kill;

'I then broke left and looked over my squadron. I was then hit by another aeroplane from below, and I supposed it was an enemy "self-blaster". I learned later, however, that it was 2Lt Grady Laseter (in P-38L 44-23935). He was evidently hit, or in some kind of trouble, for he was out of formation, flying in the opposite direction to the rest of the squadron. My aeroplane was on fire and I was forced to bail out. My left wing and both tail booms had been severed from the rest of the aircraft.

'I landed in the water near some Japanese shipping, and after nine hours in the water, I reached the west coast of Leyte Island. I was strafed twice while in the water – once by a destroyer and once by a lone "Tony". I suffered a hit in the hand by the destroyer's fire, and first, second and third

P-38L-1 '142' *Strictly Laffs!!* was the usual mount of 2Lt Henry Toll in late 1944. Coincidentally, there was also a Lightning with the same name that served with the 433rd FS later in the war (*Hoxie*)

Bombs are off-loaded from a barge on Leyte for use by the 475th FG (*Hoxie*)

Capt Fred Champlin flew 175 combat missions with the 431st, scoring nine kills in total – including five in barely six weeks over the Philippines in November-December 1944 (*Author*)

degree burns on the face, neck and right arm due to the crash. It took me until 10 December to get back to my outfit (via the Filipino guerilla network).'

Small actions continued to be fought throughout November, sending V Fighter Command victory scores up in fits and starts. Two days after Perry Dahl had claimed his seventh victory and then been obliged to run for his life through the Leyte jungle, the 431st FS fought a small, but significant, action while patrolling over Allied naval vessels operating in Leyte Gulf.

Capt Fred Champlin, who was leading 'Hades Red Flight' on this mission, was an old hand in the squadron, having scored four confirmed victories between September and December 1943. Holding a similar position to the 432nd's Perry Dahl in the central core of pilots in the 431st FS, he had been waiting almost 11 months to 'make ace'. Champlin's chance would come on 12 November 1944, when he would find that his duty included protecting American Navy vessels, as well as destroying his fifth and sixth Japanese aircraft;

'We took off from Buri Strip at 0630 hrs. Our mission was to protect a naval force in Leyte Gulf from aerial attack. During the two hours of patrolling, we were given continual plots to the south and east. After the last plot, we returned to the convoy at a height of 9000 ft. When we were almost on top of the convoy, I spotted three enemy aircraft approaching the ships from the northeast at our altitude. I immediately turned into them and recognised them as a (Ki-48) "Lily" twin-engined bomber, escorted by two "Oscars". I made a head-on pass at the "Oscars", which pulled up and around to the rear of my flight. This manoeuvre left the "Lily" alone. I turned to the left and closed on the "Lily" from 45 degrees astern. When well within range I fired a short burst, and the "Lily" immediately burst into flames and crashed in the ocean.

'I then noticed that the "Oscars" were closing on my last man. I made a sharp 180-degree turn and came at them head-on. When almost in range, they both "split-essed". I nosed straight over after the first. My second short burst hit him in the belly and he burst into flames, crashing into the sea. The pilot bailed out but his parachute did not fill with air. My last man followed the second "Oscar" through his "split-s" and scored a hit. This last enemy aeroplane started burning and crashed in the ocean. 2Lt James A Moreing accomplished this victory. I circled the area for several more minutes, but no more enemy aircraft were in sight. I then returned to base and landed at Buri Strip at 0915 hrs.'

Another local patrol in the afternoon netted four J1M 'Jack' fighters for the 431st FS, including two that fell to McGuire, one for Capt Robert 'Pappy' Cline and the fourth for Col W T Hudnell, who was flying as a guest pilot with the unit. These kills took McGuire's tally up to 28 confirmed victories, who was beginning to feel the frustration of competing with Maj Richard Bong, who had taken his score to 36 confirmed kills when he had destroyed two 'Zekes' 24 hours earlier.

It was at this point that somebody high up in the FEAF had the bright idea that public relations would benefit from Bong and McGuire flying together on operations. Thus, the two great rivals would often fly together, and even bunk together, for the rest of Bong's time in combat, which lasted until the third week of December. This PR 'dream team' turned out to be a disaster for the 475th FG, as the pressure of striving to be the top-scoring American ace of all time rasped the nerves of all who came into contact with either Bong or McGuire, and in turn soured the already strained relationship that existed between the two pilots.

CLIMAX IN THE PHILIPPINES

The 433rd FS arrived at Tacloban a few days after the 431st and 432nd FSs, by which point the latter two units had already commenced operations in earnest. Capt Campbell Wilson had taken command of the 433rd from Capt Warren Lewis in August, and he led the unit on its first patrol over Leyte on 14 November.

Five days would pass before the 433rd FS managed to claim its first kill. This honour fell to 1Lt Pierre Schoener on the afternoon of the 19th, when he shot down a dive-bomber that he identified as a 'Val' south of Dulag.

Five-kill ace 1Lt Calvin Wire led the squadron's last mission of the day when he took four P-38s out on a patrol of the local area around Dulag. The formation's fighter controller directed Wire's flight towards another group of friendly fighters that were already embroiled in a dogfight with Japanese aircraft. The ace described his claims for two 'Oscars' destroyed (the final kills of his combat tour) in his after action report;

'Unable to find this action, we patrolled the west coast of Leyte Island, and at 1615 hrs, while heading southeast, sighted eight single-engined Japanese fighters heading due south. There were six above and in no particular formation, merely bunched. About 1000 ft below them, and to the rear, were two others. Both ourselves and the six Japanese fighters

America's two top-ranking aces of all time, Majs Tom McGuire and Dick Bong, were briefly billeted together at Dulag during the campaign in the Philippines. PR types in the FEAF thought that the pairing up of the aces would play well with the American public back home, and senior officers were convinced that the men would benefit from flying with each other. However, McGuire and Bong did not get on and the 475th FG suffered accordingly (*Author*)

Capt 'Pappy' Cline flew P-38L-1 '135' *PAPPY'S Birr-die* thoughout the Philippine campaign. Cline's P-38J-15 42-104038 had also featured this nickname during the first six months of 1944 (*Author*)

Capt 'Bo' Reeves' P-38L-1 44-26187 *EL Tornado* is seen some months after the capture of the Philippines. For some reason the six-kill ace was given the CO's number for his aircraft, while Maj Cline, who was commanding the unit at the time, made do with number '135' (*Author*)

above were at 14,000 ft, and we were approaching this formation from about "five o'clock". When we were nearly within range, the two aeroplanes below the main group apparently saw us and went into 45-degree dives straight ahead.

'About 15 seconds later one of the six spotted us and signalled to the others by rocking his wings. At this signal, four of the "Oscars" climbed steeply, whilst the one on the extreme left went into a gradual level turn and the one on the far right executed a slight turn to the right. I went after the latter aircraft, opening fire at about 200 yards. The Nip then rolled over into a "split-s", but I was able to follow him using my diving flaps (fitted to all P-38Ls). Closing to about 100 yards, I fired a long burst of about two seconds. He went straight down and crashed into the water at full speed. This action ended between the Camotes Islands and Bulacan (on Leyte Island).

'We continued our patrol, going south along Leyte's west coast. At about 1625 hrs we observed a single bogey headed north and flying at

433rd FS crewmen Angus McMurchie and George Rath pose with their charge, P-38J-15 42-104035, which was assigned to unit CO, and seven-kill ace, Maj Warren Lewis. The longevity of this aircraft was remarkable, as the fighter served in the frontline from January 1944 until the eve of the Philippine invasion (*Hanks*)

approximately our level. I turned immediately, got on his tail and approached to within 200 yards before he saw us. In an effort to flee into the overcast, he turned straight up, but I followed him, closing to within 50 yards during this manoeuvre. My 20 mm fire smashed into his engine and cockpit, whereupon he burst into flame, spun on into the ground and exploded south of Baybay.'

The 433rd FS also ran into several wild fights on 24 November, emerging with one Zero and four other single-engined fighters identified as 'Tonys' or 'Jacks' claimed destroyed. The latter fighters could have been the first examples of the new N1K 'George' naval fighter encountered by the 475th FG, as this aircraft was in the throes of being introduced into IJN service on the Philippine front. The 433rd FS's afternoon patrol of four P-38s had ran into 'Georges' of the 701st Hikotai, and two Lightnings had soon been forced down by the agile Japanese interceptor – both pilots were eventually recovered, however. In return, the 701st Hikotai lost its veteran CO, and nine-kill ace, Cdr Aya-o Shirane. His demise has been studied by Japanese historians postwar, and they are convinced that his N1K Shiden fell victim to an attack by a 433rd FS P-38.

DECEMBER BATTLES

The bitter fighting over the Philippines continued into December 1944, with the 433rd FS scoring a further 25 kills. 1Lt John 'Jack' Purdy was one of those pilots to enjoy success during this period, claiming no fewer than six victories in three clashes with Japanese aircraft. Having downed an 'Oscar' for his first victory in May, he destroyed two 'Vals' for his second and third kills on 5 December whilst leading a patrol of four P-38s between Albuera and Baybay, on Leyte.

Six days later, Purdy 'made ace' with two 'Oscars' shot down and another damaged, before he in turn was forced to bail out of his P-38L when he ran out of fuel over Cabugan Grande Island. He managed to make it back to base that same day after hitching lifts aboard a Catalina flying-boat and an L-4 Grasshopper.

Four days prior to Purdy achieving acedom, the FEAF's fighter force was tasked with protecting new Allied landings in Leyte's Ormoc Bay. In the fierce fighting which ensued, V Fighter Command pilots claimed more than 50 Japanese aircraft shot down in a day-long series of engagements. Almost every American fighter ace in-theatre added to his score, and the 475th FG had one of its greatest days when it was credited with the destruction of 26 enemy aircraft.

In various clashes which took place from early morning to late afternoon, the fighters of the FEAF parried every thrust and inflicted frustrating losses on JAAF and IJN formations attempting to disrupt the invasion. The 49th FG's Maj Jerry Johnson claimed four victories during a morning patrol when he shot down three 'Oscars', which crashed almost simultaneously into Ormoc Bay, and a 'Helen' bomber in the space of just five minutes.

Col MacDonald was the 475th FG's top scorer on 7 December, claiming three 'Jack' fighters between 1125 hrs and 1430 hrs during the course of two flights. Lt Col Meryl Smith (in P-38L-1 44-23945) also enjoyed success against the J2M fighter, claiming a pair to take his tally to nine kills on the same morning mission that MacDonald had been

Lt Col Meryl M Smith was a dynamic leader, having joined the 475th FG from the 35th FG shortly after the new group was established in July 1943. He went on to claim nine victories, and led the 475th when Col MacDonald was on enforced leave in August-October 1944. Smith downed two 'Jacks' in a late morning sortie over Ormoc Bay on 7 December 1944, but was then posted missing in action during a second patrol in the same area less than three hours later (*Hoxie*)

credited with one destroyed. These would be his last victories, however, for Smith was posted missing following another clash with 'Jacks' over Ponson Island at 1430 hrs that same day.

1Lt Joe Forster of the 432nd FS had been the first 475th FG pilot to see action on the 7th when, at 0750 hrs, his flight had run into a Ki-46 'Dinah' reconnaissance aircraft snooping around west of Dulag. His fire caused one of the aircraft's engines to smoke badly, although the 'Dinah' escaped when it flew into heavy ground fog at low altitude – the veteran ace knew that it would have been suicidal to have continued the pursuit. Although certain that the Ki-46 was doomed, Forster had to be content with only a probable victory.

Three hours later, on his second patrol of the morning (the same one that McDonald and Smith participated in), Forster was more certain about the end result of his attacks. Leading the second flight of four 432nd FS aircraft, he managed to get in behind a Zero that was subsequently observed to fall burning into the sea between Ponson and Poro Islands. Forster then hunted down yet another Ki-46 after a squadronmate had burned out his guns trying to bring it down. Slipping in behind the fleeing reconnaissance aircraft, he opened fire from very close range and knocked out one of its engines. Clearly unable to escape, the Japanese pilot crash-landed on Ponson Island. These victories boosted Forster's tally to eight kills.

Dick Bong and Tom McGuire flew together several times during the day, and each pilot scored two victories. Bong claimed a Ki-21 'Sally' bomber and a 'Tojo' fighter during an afternoon patrol, while McGuire got an 'Oscar' in the morning and a 'Tojo' in the afternoon. Both pilots witnessed and confirmed at least one victory for the other, and 1Lt Floyd Fulkerson witnessed one victory for each pilot, as well as confirming a 'Tojo' for himself.

As an incidental point, Fulkerson emphatically believed that McGuire was a superior pilot to Bong. This may very well have been the case, but it

Capt Bill Weaver and 1Lt Ken Hart of the 431st FS pose beneath the kill tally applied to the former's P-38L-1. Despite his fighter bearing four swastikas, Weaver was only ever officially credited with two victories while flying P-40s in the Mediterranean. He failed to add to his tally in the Southwest Pacific theatre. Hart, however, finished the war with eight kills (*Author*)

1Lt Hart's P-38L-1 44-25863 carried
the squadron number '111'. The
aircraft is seen here prior to it being
adorned with the ace's *Peewee V*
titling, as well as the devil's head
motif on the nose (*Author*)

was quite the rage at the time to compare Bong favourably or unfavourably
to various other leading pilots in-theatre – yet another factor that perhaps
contributed to friction between Bong and McGuire. Indeed, soon after
7 December Bong packed up his kit and moved out of the tent that he had
briefly shared with McGuire.

The 431st FS's 1Lt Ken Hart claimed two 'Oscars' during a late
afternoon patrol on the 7th, thus making him the 475th FG's newest ace.
Although his after action report was very brief, it accurately revealed the
sort of fighting the group's pilots had participated in during this day of
heavy action;

'Capt Champlin, with 2Lt Martin on his wing, 1Lt Provencio as
element leader and myself as the No 4 man took off from Dulag at 1600
hrs. While flying south near Leyte, we spotted a "Zeke" to the west of us,
heading north at about 8000 ft. We gave chase, and Capt Champlin shot
him down in flames from dead astern off the north tip of Cebu. Flying
north at 4000 ft near the Camotes Islands, we sighted and gave chase to an
"Oscar" at 6000 ft, heading southwest. At a height of about 3000 ft, I fired
from 0 to 30 degrees deflection from astern, observing a flash of flame on
the right side of the engine and the Nip rolled over and went in just east of
Olango Island.

'At approximately 1800 hrs we tagged an "Oscar" at 6000 ft, headed
northwest, and chased him to the deck. He broke to the right and I fired
from 30 to 60 degrees deflection, scoring hits on his engine and cockpit,
setting him afire. He crashed in flames into the Camotes Sea at about 1810
hrs. We then proceeded to home, landing at 1830 hrs.'

2Lt Chase Brenizer of the 433rd FS registered the 475th FG's final
victory of 7 December when he claimed a 'Helen' bomber shot down over
the sea off Leyte at 1750 hrs.

The day ended on a poignant note for Col MacDonald when he and
another pilot sortied just before dusk, after most of the missions had been
completed for the day, to look for any sign of Lt Col Meryl Smith. They
searched the Camotes Sea for an hour at altitudes from 1000 ft down to

Aces High! Capt Fred Champlin and 1Lts Ken Hart, John Pietz and Frank Monk clown around with Champlin's pet monkey on Leyte in late 1944. All four pilots had become aces with the 431st FS by the time the Philippines campaign had been won (*Author*)

wave-top height without success, before landing back at base at 1810 hrs. Smith was never found.

GROUP RIVALRY

The rivalry between the 49th and 475th FGs, which were co-located on Leyte in November-December 1944, was at its height during the Philippines campaign. Both groups scored heavily during the invasion, and by war's end the 49th FG came out on top with 664 victories thanks to its early war service. The 475th totalled 552 kills, its pilots having set some impressive records during its brief 24 months in the frontline.

Dick Bong, who flew with both groups (although he was officially attached to V Fighter Command during his time with the 475th FG)

2Lt Chase Brenizer is seen here with his P-38J-15 42-104494 *CHASE'S ACE* in which he claimed three Japanese aircraft destroyed for the 433rd FS. The last of these fell to him during the great 7 December 1944 battle over Leyte. Brenizer was reportedly killed in a flying accident sometime after he left the 475th FG (*Author*)

Maj McGuire stands alongside his *PUDGY (V)* in a photograph that was snapped by a groundcrewman on 20 December 1944, when his score stood at 31 (*Bates*)

scored his 40th, and last, victory (a Ki-43) on the afternoon of 17 December when he and 2Lt Fulkerson were patrolling over the new Allied beachhead on Mindoro Island. He had been presented with the Medal of Honor by Gen MacArthur five days earlier, and he would be sent home for good as America's premier ace just prior to Christmas.

Driven on by the attention lavished on his great rival, Tom McGuire was straining at the bit to surpass Bong, and his exploits over Clark Field almost saw him snatch top spot.

The 475th FG played a key role in the first attacks on the airfield complex at Clark Field, which had been in Japanese hands since Luzon had fallen in early 1942. The 72 hours of fierce fighting that took place in this area between 24 and 26 December 1944 effectively broke the back of JAAF and IJN air power in the Southwest Pacific.

Air battles on Christmas Eve saw 33 Japanese fighters attempting to defend Clark Field fall to P-47 pilots from the 348th FG, whilst on 25 December the P-38s of the 49th and 475th FGs accounted for 40 more

431st FS pose outside the unit's briefing hut at Dulag. They are, in the back row, from left to right, 1Lts John Tillley and Harold Gray, Capt Fred Champlin and 1Lt Ken Hart, and in the front row, again from left to right, are 1Lts Louis DuMontier, John 'Rabbit' Pietz, Horace 'Bo' Reeves and Merle Pearson (*Author*)

enemy aircraft. For the latter group, the 431st once again scored the lion's share of the kills, with 18 aircraft being claimed for the loss of three P-38s and two pilots. Both 2Lt Robert Koeck (in P-38L-1 44-24846) and 1Lt Enrique Provencio (in P-38L-1 44-24889) were killed over Clark Field, but squadronmate 1Lt Floyd Fulkerson, who claimed two 'Jack' fighters before he was downed, successfully evaded capture.

1Lt John 'Rabbit' Pietz also shot down two J2M fighters on Christmas Day to take his tally to five victories, while 1Lt John Tilley downed yet another 'Jack' to leave him just one short of acedom. Unlike Fulkerson, who would end the war with four kills, Tilley would get his crucial fifth kill just 24 hours later.

Maj Tom McGuire, to adopt the vernacular of the time, 'went wild' and successfully attacked three Zeros in the space of just 15 minutes before his guns were literally burned out by the long bursts that he had used in his zeal to down as many Japanese aircraft as possible. He was in the process of attacking a fourth enemy fighter down near the ground when all of his guns ceased to function. Out of options, McGuire ordered his wingman, 1Lt Alvin Neal, to shoot down the frustratingly vulnerable target.

The 432nd FS added six kills to the total, one of which provided 1Lt Joe Forster with his ninth, and last, victory, the 433rd claimed just one 'Zeke' destroyed and Col MacDonald got two 'Jacks' and a Zero to increase his tally to 24.

A repeat operation over the same area the following morning saw McGuire fly his most successful mission in terms of aerial victories, the group's leading ace knocking down four 'Zekes' in just ten minutes near Clark Field. His score now stood at 38, and he was seemingly within touching distance of Bong's 40 kills.

Current or future aces Capt Fred Champlin and 1Lts 'Bo' Reeves and John Tilley also claimed a 'Zeke' apiece, with Tilley's kill making him the group's newest ace.

The Clark Field clash of 26 December proved to be the last great aerial battle of the Philippines campaign, and although other victories would be claimed by the 475th FG into 1945, the group's pilots would never again encounter massed ranks of Japanese aircraft as they had done in 1943-44.

All three of these 475th aces had perished by early 1945. Lt Col Meryl Smith (centre) went missing during the fighting on 7 December 1944 after being bounced by 'Jacks', Capt Henry Condon (left) of the 431st FS was shot down by ground fire whilst attacking a target in Manila in P-38L-1 44-24843 on 2 January 1945, and 1Lt Frank Lent was lost on 1 December 1944 after his tour had expired. Having finished flying with the 475th FG, he managed to wangle a hop in a new photo-reconnaissance F-6D-10 Mustang (44-14621) and promptly crashed it into the sea off Lae (*Author*)

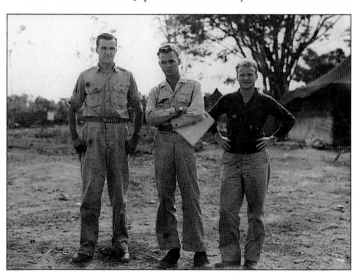

SOUTHEAST ASIA AND BEYOND

January 1945 started off on a brisk note for the 475th FG when its last attack on the Clark Field complex in strength on New Year's Day netted the group three victories, as well as six more for the 49th FG. This proved to be the last sizeable action to be seen by V Fighter Command in the Philippines, aside from the astonishing Medal of Honor mission in which Capt William Shomo of the 82nd TRS/71st PRG claimed seven victories in a single action in his F-6D Mustang over northern Luzon on 11 January.

The fighter groups in the Philippines were still blissfully unaware that Japanese aerial resistance in the region had collapsed, leaving the 49th FG, in particular, unable to cash in on its exclusive assignment of the previously lucrative hunting ground over Luzon by V Fighter Command chief Brig Gen Paul 'Squeeze' Wurtsmith.

One of the 475th pilots who did well on 1 January over Clark was Col Charles MacDonald, who shot down a 'Dinah' and a 'Tojo' to boost his tally to 26 aerial victories. The group CO had taken command of a five-aeroplane flight from the 432nd FS, MacDonald relishing this position at the head of a formation of P-38s on a fighter sweep. His after action report contains some interesting details about the mission;

'We approached the target at 18,000 ft, but let down to 14,000 ft because of the overcast. I sighted a lone "Dinah" coming in from the northwest at 12,000 ft. I tried for a head-on attack but he was in a slight dive, and turning. I could only get a 40-degree angle-off shot in. I fired an extremely short burst with two radii lead, then turned to get a stern shot, but discovered that he was already on fire. He rolled over and went into a vertical dive. As his speed and the fire increased, he disintegrated, shedding large pieces before he crashed.

'The next enemy aeroplane to go down was a fighter, which was destroyed by the element leader (Capt Paul Lucas) of a flight of four P-38s over Clark Field. I then observed two P-38s (from the 49th FG) destroy another fighter ten miles west of Clark Field.

'I sighted a single enemy fighter at 4000 ft, heading west, and dived down on him from the stern. A series of short bursts set him flaming. This enemy aeroplane, which was a "Tojo", crashed eight to ten miles west of Clark Field. Immediately after this I saw a parachute descending, and thinking it might be one of ours, I investigated. It turned out to be an extremely nonchalant Nip in a dark green flying suit, floating down with his legs crossed and his elbow propped up on the shrouds. I returned to home base via Mindoro, where two aeroplanes from my formation landed for gas.'

As mentioned in this report, the other pilot from the 432nd FS to claim a kill on 1 January was Capt Paul Lucas, who shot down a Zero for

432nd FS CO Capt Henry Condon was downed by ground fire while strafing a train on 2 January 1945. He was flying Col MacDonald's P-38L-1 44-24843 *PUTT PUTT MARU* at the time, and had been one of the group's early veterans to rise to command rank (*Hoxie*)

his sixth, and final, victory – he would be killed in action exactly two weeks later.

Tragedy struck the 432nd FS during the early morning sweep sent out on 2 January when squadron CO, and five-kill ace, Capt Henry Condon was shot down and killed whilst at the controls of Col MacDonald's P-38L-1 44-24843. The unit had originally been tasked with escorting B-25s that had been sent to bomb Porac and Floridablanca Airfield, but when the P-38 pilots lost contact with the bombers in the heavy overcast, Condon took his 11 Lightnings to the target area independently of the Mitchells.

A few miles north of Manila, Condon led two flights down to strafe a train, which exploded after he passed over it. Moments after Condon attempted to turn to make another pass on the target, his fighter began to trail smoke. Other pilots from the 432nd FS then saw Condon open the canopy, probably in preparation for bailing out, but the Lightning crashed into a field some ten miles north of Manila before the ace had had the chance to take to his parachute.

Sadly, Henry Condon, who had served with the 475th since June 1943, would not be the group's only ace to be killed in action in January 1945.

DEATH OF TOM McGUIRE

As January progressed, V Fighter Command pilots began to grow frustrated at the lack of action in the skies over the Philippines. Perhaps the most frustrated of them all was Maj Thomas B McGuire, who had been only three kills short of becoming the all time American ace of aces since 26 December 1944. To make matters worse for the 475th FG, the new division of territory between it and the 49th FG saw the latter group better positioned to oppose any Japanese aggression thanks to it being given responsibility for the northern part of Luzon, where JAAF units were still active. The triangle reserved for the 475th between Mindanao and Mindoro was now something of a backwater for the Japanese.

As if this was not bad enough for McGuire, his anxiety was further fuelled by the knowledge that he would be rotated home in the very near future. The ace had already been on operations for almost two years, and he had suffered wounds in combat as well as tropical illnesses such as malaria. The only way McGuire could possibly stay in-theatre was to accept a more senior position within the 475th, and it was unlikely that he could go any higher than the job he now held, which was group operations officer.

These matters weighed heavily on his mind when he organised 'Daddy Special' flight, consisting of four 431st FS P-38Ls, for a sweep of Fabrica airfield on Negros Island on the morning of 7 January 1945. Officially, squadron mission number 1-668 took off at 0620 hrs, with McGuire in the lead position in P-38L-1 44-24845 '112', which was usually flown by

either Capt Fred Champlin or 1Lt Hal Gray – he had all but worn *PUDGY (V)* out, having flown it very hard during the previous weeks of combat. Capt Ed Weaver was assigned 1Lt Tom Oxford's P-38L-1 44-25878 '122', and was flying on McGuire's wing, while Thirteenth Air Force veteran Maj Jack Rittmayer (who had four kills to his name) led the second element in 1Lt Rohrer's P-38J-15 43-28836 '128', and 2Lt Doug Thropp was 'tail end Charlie' in P-38J-15 43-28525 '130'.

An undercast prevented the pilots from observing any activity on Negros, so McGuire led his formation down to 1700 ft. The flight then circled boldly over Fabrica at an attitude of belligerence, hoping to provoke spirited response from Japanese aircraft on the airfield. However, nothing seemed to be happening at Fabrica, so McGuire set course for airstrips in the western part of the island. Shortly after leaving Fabrica, Weaver called out what he thought was a 'Zeke 52' about 1000 yards ahead of them at an altitude of 500 ft. McGuire immediately started a diving turn to the left to trap the enemy fighter.

Unbeknown to the Americans at the time, the 'Zeke 52' was actually an 'Oscar' of the 54th Sentai, piloted by combat veteran Wt Off Akira Sugimoto. He had been flying a frustrating mission over weather-obscured seas in search of an American supply convoy. When he spotted the P-38s trying to encircle him, he began to turn tightly to the left himself so as to get onto the tail of 2Lt Thropp's P-38.

Four 431st FS aircraft are seen on a patrol from Dulag in mid January 1945. The pilot of P-38L-1 44-25639 '126' is six-kill ace 1Lt John Pietz, while P-38L-5 44-25878 '122' was normally flown by 1Lt Tom Oxford, although five-kill ace 1Lt John Tilley was at the controls when this photograph was taken. 1Lt Louis DuMontier is flying his P-38L-5 44-25439 *MADU V* and nine-kill ace Capt Fred Champlin is in his P-38L-5 44-25056 *EILEEN ANNE* (*Author*)

Maj McGuire's *PUDGY (V)* is seen soon after he had scored his final kill. Note the prepared space ready for his next victory (*Bates*)

In his eagerness to score a kill, McGuire had failed to order his formation to jettison the still partly-filled external tanks hung beneath the wings of their Lightnings prior to attacking the lone enemy fighter. Thus, Sugimoto in his nimble Ki-43 was able to easily turn inside the P-38s and begin a firing pass on Thropp. Yet despite his clear advantage over his foes, the Japanese pilot inexplicably missed with every shot he fired!

Shaken by the threat posed to his wingman, Maj Rittmayer tried to turn his overloaded Lightning in behind the pugnacious 'Oscar'. Sugimoto responded by simply tightening his turn to get in behind Rittmayer's heavily laden P-38, which was flying low and slow over the lush Negros landscape.

Capt Weaver survived the mission, and later wrote a report that outlined what happened next;

'I radioed that the "Zeke" was directly behind us, and Maj Rittmayer, in the No 4 position, fired a burst sufficient to make the enemy turn even more tightly and lose 2Lt Thropp. That put the "Zeke" in range and inside of me, in the No 2 position. I radioed Maj McGuire that I was being attacked, and increased my turn, diving slightly. The enemy stayed with me, but I was now inside and a little below my leader.

'At this time Maj McGuire, attempting to get a shot at my attacker, increased his turn tremendously. His aeroplane snap-rolled to the left and stopped in an inverted position, with the nose down about 30 degrees. Because of the attitude of my aeroplane, I then lost sight of him momentarily. A second later I saw the explosion and fire of his crash. The "Zeke" broke off his attack just before Maj McGuire's crash, and climbed to the north. It is my opinion that the enemy did not at any time change his attack from me to my leader. I believe that Maj McGuire's crash was caused by his violent attempt to thwart my attacker, although it is possible that the major was hit by ground fire, which had now begun.'

Whilst Sugimoto concentrated on Rittmayer and Weaver, Thropp had somehow managed to come around enough in the ever tightening circle to get in behind the 'Oscar' and fire a three-second burst. McGuire crashed moments later, and the plucky Japanese pilot took this opportunity to make good his escape to the north. However, his aircraft had perhaps already been damaged by fire from one of the American fighters because he duly made a crash-landing and was immediately shot dead by Filipino partisans.

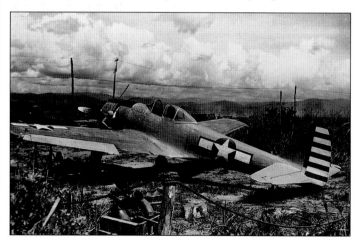

This airworthy Ki-43 'Oscar' was found abandoned at Hollandia following the Allied invasion in April 1944. The Japanese fighter had almost certainly been a part of the 77th Sentai prior to its capture. Stripped back to bare metal and nicknamed *RACOON Special* (the call-sign of the 8th FS, which also flew the fighter), the aircraft was test flown by P-38 pilots from the 432nd FS. Fifth Air Force records hint that the 'Oscar' may have subsequently been sent to the USA for more thorough testing (*Author*)

A few minutes after Sugimoto fled north, the surviving American pilots believed that the fighter they had originally engaged had impudently returned to attack them again when a Ki-84 'Frank' of the 71st Sentai, flown by Sgt Mizonori Fukuda appeared on the scene. It had intercepted the Lightnings from the opposite direction in which Sugimoto had fled, and Fukuda had used the element of surprise to get onto the tails of the three P-38s that were now at last rid of their drop tanks.

With the latter encumbrance gone, the 431st FS pilots responded more effectively to the attack, but not effectively enough to stop Fukuda from firing an accurate 90-degree shot that brought down Maj Rittmayer's P-38 (killing the pilot) and damaged 2Lt Thropp's fighter. In return, Weaver and Thropp damaged the 'Frank' sufficiently enough to write it off when Fukuda crash-landed at Manalpa airfield.

The death of Tom McGuire struck a heavy blow to American morale in the Philippines when news of his death was announced. He had been the symbol of invulnerability, especially with the rotation of Dick Bong back home less than three weeks earlier, and in spite of his controversial nature, McGuire was universally regarded as the spirit of valour in the skies in the Pacific. His fearlessness was inspiring, but in the end he was vulnerable to the law of averages which plagued all fighter pilots on operations.

THE END IN THE PHILIPPINES

It was a remarkable repeat of history when American forces landed in Lingayen Gulf on 9 January 1945, for the Japanese had used much the same route to conquer Luzon in the opening stages of the Pacific War some three years earlier. Now the enemy they had vanquished was following in their footsteps as the Allies completely reversed the situation in the Philippines. And just as Japanese forces had swept into Manila in early 1942, the Americans were now threatening to take back the capital in 1945. Although Manila fell soon after the invasion, Luzon itself was not declared secure until June 1945. By then, of course, the Philippines had long stopped supporting the purposes of the Japanese Empire.

Coincidentally, two days after the loss of Maj Thomas McGuire, the entire FEAF was committed to the invasion of Luzon, including the fighter groups assigned to other areas of the Philippines.

On the day that US troops stepped ashore at Lingayen Gulf, four P-38s of the 432nd FS flew a disappointing dive-bombing mission against a bridge north of Manila, as was recorded in the squadron's operational diary;

'Our first bombing mission of the month was flown today, and it was a dismal failure. Our task was to skip-bomb a bridge at Calumpit, on Luzon. Four aeroplanes took off from Dulag at 0615 hrs, carrying one 2000-lb bomb each. When our P-38s reached the target area, the skies above the bridge were already overcrowded with friendly aircraft. B-25s were strafing the railroad from an altitude of 25 ft, before heading off the target directly towards our Lightnings. Elsewhere, the roads were being strafed in both directions by A-20s. Anxious to avoid us being hit by a medium bomber, our flight leader continued on past our original target and led us in to bomb a bridge approximately one mile above Melolos.

'It was quite evident from the results of the bombing that our pilots needed a little more practice, as two bombs fell short, one overshot and one was jettisoned by accident. All aeroplanes landed back at Dulag at 1245 hrs.

'All the aerial activity up in Luzon today was due to the fact that our troops were making a landing at Lingayen. At last we have a foothold on Luzon, the enemy's principal base in the Philippines.'

With little aerial opposition now to speak of, the 475th FG began loading up its P-38s with bombs – on the mission just detailed, each of the four P-38s carried a single one-ton weapon. Lt Gen Ennis Whitehead had recently become head of the Fifth Air Force, and one of his new innovations was the fitment of heavier bomb loads to P-38s in order for them to be more effective in the ground attack mission. Col MacDonald lauded this decision, stating after the war that it was one of the most effective, and original, orders issued by a commander during the Pacific campaign.

But just as the P-38 was set to embrace a new mission in the Pacific, units operating the Lockheed fighter began to feel the effects of a shortage in airframes in-theatre. This problem was nothing new to the Fifth Air Force, as throughout 1943 and well into 1944, the Lightning had been the US fighter of choice for USAAF commanders worldwide, yet it had been produced in far fewer numbers than any other American single-seat fighter type. When an overall reduction in demand for P-38s in Europe lessened the strain on the Pacific units, the relatively modest demands in the Southwest Pacific were at last satisfied in the summer of 1944. However, for some inexplicable reason the shortage occurred once again, and this time worse than ever, in early 1945.

Fortunately, with the virtual defeat of Japanese air power in the region, the FEAF did not suffer too badly due to the reduced number of P-38s in-theatre. Nevertheless, the shortage affected the 475th FG to the degree that its squadrons had to put up mixed flights of say two 'Hades' and two 'Clover' P-38s in order to fulfil convoy cover duty during this period simply because no single unit in the group could consistently muster four serviceable Lightnings at any one time.

Although the FEAF was suffering its own problems at this time, these were nothing compared to those besetting the enemy. Surviving Japanese forces in the Philippines were both fragmented and undersupplied because of the Allied air and naval dominance in-theatre. Slowly, enemy troops were forced south into isolated pockets of resistance and to the north through the Balete Pass, where they could only hope to repeat the previous American delaying tactics of previous battles fought in 1942.

One objective of special interest to US forces was the resort town of Baguio, situated midway up the western coast of Luzon. Aircrew flying over Baguio spotted golf courses, swimming pools and other recreational facilities which ensured that they did not inflict serious damage to the town, lest they destroy a prime rest and leave spot for future use!

The 432nd FS was spared the possibility of inadvertently causing damage to Baguio on 17 January when four of its P-38s were each scheduled to drop a 2000-lb pound bomb on a road south of the town, only to have the mission scrubbed by weather. The Lightning pilots went after the alternate target of Silay airstrip, on Negros Island, instead, only to find that none of the bombs exploded when they were dropped. In frustration, they then strafed the strip, with unobserved results. Flak over this target had claimed the unit's Capt Paul Lucas two days earlier, and although the six-kill ace had managed to crash-land his damaged

Six-kill ace Capt Paul Lucas was another veteran pilot from the 432nd FS to succumb to ground fire in the final months of the war. He was shot down on 15 January 1945 (*Hoxie*)

Bearing the 475th HQ number '101', this P-38L was usually flown by the group's deputy commander – either Lt Cols Meryl Smith or John Loisel, the latter being promoted to fill this position following Smith's death in combat on 7 December 1944 (*Ethell*)

fighter (P-38L-1 44-25336), he was found dead in the cockpit of his machine by friendly Filipino partisans when they ran to help the downed American pilot.

The squadron again had no luck when sent to bomb Baguio on 21 January, poor weather over the target area obliging seven 'Clover' P-38 pilots to take their 14 1000-lb bombs to an alternate target on Negros Island. A pier was completely destroyed at Bacolod, and the P-38s strafed buildings and other structures in the area.

Baguio was finally bombed with more success the following day when flights from both 'Hades' and 'Clover' squadrons attacked the nearby airstrip. After-mission assessment judged that the airfield, and its runways, were now inoperable for Japanese aircraft that could have used the base to oppose the impending US invasion of the region.

Poor weather further impeded operations to some extent over the next few days, limiting flights to local convoy patrol or short-range armed reconnaissance missions. Maj John Loisel had inherited the job of group operations officer following McGuire's death, and he led the 432nd FS, which he had previously commanded, on a convoy patrol south of Leyte on 27 January. He took off at 0715 hrs in typically rainy weather with three other 'Clover Squadron' P-38s for a three-hour flight, and was back at the sodden airfield at Dulag by 1045 hrs.

The mission would have been entirely routine except that Loisel parked at the end of the slippery runway to observe the landings of his relatively inexperienced flight members. Sure enough, 2Lt Arnold W Larsen skidded badly on his landing run (in P-38L-1 44-23921) and struck a helpless Loisel, sat in Col MacDonald's fourth *PUTT PUTT MARU* (P-38L-5 44-25643), as the skidding Lightning ran head on into the commander's aircraft. Neither man was hurt, but both P-38s were written off and sent over to the 10th Service Squadron for disposition.

This particular *PUTT PUTT MARU* had only been in service for about three weeks, thus having what must have been the shortest service life of any P-38 flown by Col MacDonald. His reaction was very mild, considering the loss of one of his precious P-38s – after some understandably negative comment by the CO when he was first told about the accident, he simply commented, 'Johnny should have been more careful, and not have sat so close to that crowded and slippery runway'. MacDonald was known for being a tough commander, but he was also ultimately fair.

The 121st, and last, aerial victory scored by the 433rd FS during the Pacific War had come a few days before the accident, on 24 January, when 1Lt LeRoy Ross confirmed a Japanese fighter shot down over a convoy just east of Negros Island. The unit report of the action is typically understated, but nevertheless informative;

'Patrol convoy south of Sequijor Island, completed. One "Zeke 52" definitely destroyed, our losses nil. Two "Zeke 52s" sighted, headed southeast at 9000 ft about 40 miles south of Sequijor Island. P-38s headed 90 degrees at 9000 ft. Remaining three "Zeke 52s" escaped to the southeast during combat. "Zekes" were carrying belly tanks and did not appear to be attempting to attack convoy.

'Flight leader and wingman handling high cover approached from "six o'clock" at 9000 ft, flight leader closed to 120 yards and fired short burst, causing right wing and right belly tank of enemy aircraft to explode. Enemy pilot bailed out and aeroplane crashed into water 18 miles northeast of Plaridel, Mindanao.

'En route, four-tenths scattered cumulus 4000-10,000 ft. Eight belly tanks dropped. "Zeke 52s" were painted a dark green and had large red roundels. One "Zeke" had a wide orange band running around fuselage just to rear of cockpit.'

The identification of the enemy types encountered as A6M5 Zeros was probably in error, for these fighters were more likely to have been Ki-84 Hayates, known as 'Frank' to the Allies. This victory would have been even more gratifying to Ross if he had realised at the time that he would be the last 433rd pilot to claim an enemy fighter – and one of the best Japanese types to boot.

In February the 475th FG continued with its near-daily routine of flying patrol and ground attack missions throughout the region. The

The 431st FS's armament section service machine guns and cannon at San Jose in mid February 1945. These men are, from left to right, Cpl Edward M Pierson, Sgt Patrick Antropik, TSgt Elmer Hines, SSgt Roy Paines and Cpl William Pappas, with Cpl Robert Cronk sat in the background (*Army Air Forces*)

operational diary of the 432nd FS for 2 February 1945, which noted the tedium of operations at this time, also lamented the sorry state of the unit's operational strength;

'Today's flight was a good indication of the type of missions being meted out to our squadron due to our shortage of aeroplanes. Four aeroplanes escorted C-47s to Mindoro and back. Take-off was at 0900 hrs and landing time 1530 hrs. There were nil sightings during the mission.'

On 4 February the squadron was reinforced with new personnel and a handful of replacement aircraft, which allowed it to fly nine P-38s to its new base on Mindoro over the next few days. Although routine missions continued during this period, the unit's pilots hoped for more action in the immediate future. And they were not disappointed when Col MacDonald visited the 432nd to fly with the squadron on 13 February.

The CO led a flight of five P-38s on a bomber escort mission that began at 0730 hrs, the P-38s departing from Elmore Field, on Mindoro, to cover the 'heavies' as they went after Japanese shipping off the coast of China. Although a number of vessels were discovered in the target area, heavy cloud saved them from being attacked, and forced the bombers to jettison their loads harmlessly into the water. MacDonald, however, made the most of the situation when he sighted a Ki-57 'Topsy' transport aircraft and shot it down in flames. One horrific detail from the engagement recounted by the pilots involved upon their return to base was the sight of passengers jumping without parachutes to escape the flames and imminent crash. The destruction of this machine gave MacDonald his 27th, and final, victory.

The 431st FS found good hunting during a Navy PB4Y escort on 25 February when, just off the coast of Indochina near Cam Ranh Bay, a number of A6M2-N 'Rufe' floatplane fighters were caught in the process of taking off. Two of the Japanese aircraft boldly attacked the 12 P-38s from different directions and altitudes and were promptly shot down, whilst two others were destroyed in strafing runs on their ramps. Having destroyed all of the 'Rufes', as well as their base, the Lightning pilots then set about strafing any ship or installation along the nearby coastline.

The group also commenced napalm fire-bombing missions at the end of February, with the 432nd FS flying its first such operation on the 26th when 12 of its P-38s attacked Puerta Princessa, on Palawan Island, in preparation for a forthcoming invasion. Several hours later, four 432nd FS fighters were sent to Busuaga Island to strafe and bomb a crashed B-25 that had force-landed in a fairly intact condition. This proved to be one of the more unusual operations flown by the unit, and flight commander Capt Joe Forster subsequently reported 'a souvenir hunter couldn't have salvaged enough aluminium to make a decent set of ear-rings for his lady fair' after the four P-38s had worked over the hapless bomber.

March started much to the liking of seven-kill ace Capt Perry Dahl when he led the 432nd FS on a seven-aeroplane fighter sweep of Formosa on the 5th. This mission was the first squadron operation flown by the unit from its new base at the Clark Field complex, the group having occupied the site on 28 February. The 432nd found itself camped between airstrip No 4 and Fort Stotsenberg, and declared itself operational in just a matter of days so as to be available to fly this potentially lucrative sweep.

Dahl made the most of the opportunity when he led his P-38s down in an abortive run on what turned out to be a civilian fishing fleet. However, soon

Left and above
The 431st FS's 1Lt Floyd Fenton and
an unnamed crewman pose beside
the gaudily marked P-38L-5 44-26404
***GLOP GLOP* in early 1945 (*Author*)**

after levelling off at just 1500 ft, Dahl spotted a Ki-21 'Sally' bomber flying in the opposite direction to him at his altitude just inland from his present position. The ace quickly reversed his course and came up directly behind the enemy aircraft, whose pilot was diving frantically in a futile effort to escape the P-38. Dahl fired a few bursts that set an engine on fire and caused large pieces of the Ki-21's fuselage to fly off. The 'Sally' exploded upon hitting the ground, but to the utter amazement of the circling P-38s above it, five surviving crew members were seen to escape from the wreckage and run for cover.

The next day the Japanese welcomed the 475th FG to Clark Field by staging a rare air raid on the base. For 90 minutes in the early hours of 6 March enemy aircraft roared back and forth over the area totally unopposed since anti-aircraft defences had not yet been put in place. From 0300 hrs until 0430 hrs, the raiders sought out targets and dropped at least two sticks of bombs. However, they inflicted little physical damage of note, although they certainly frayed the nerves of the group personnel who huddled in whatever shelter they could find.

Missions continued unabated throughout March, with bomber escorts to the Southeast Asian coastline punctuating patrols and ground support operations. All the while, US troops were advancing along the western Luzon coast and east into the Cagayan valley, and on 15 March the 475th flew its first missions in support of ground forces advancing northward towards Baguio. By the end of the month, targets around Manila were also being hit as the Allies attempted to drive a wedge between the Japanese Army's northern Kembu group and the southern Shimbu group. By April, Japanese forces had become heavily fragmented, just as the US resistance in the Philippines had been three years earlier, with no hope of reinforcement or re-supply.

The 433rd FS's two ground attack missions on 28 March illustrate how the 475th FG was implementing its role as the harasser of retreating Japanese forces in the Manila area. The first mission saw P-38s attack a motor pool south of Santa Fe just after 0900 hrs, 12 1000-lb bombs hitting the target and two others damaging a building 600 yards away. Two more bombs were jettisoned in Pampanga Bay when no more suitable targets could be found. All eight P-38s involved in the operation also made two strafing runs to complete a successful mission.

Later that same afternoon, eight Lightnings from the 433rd FS dropped a further 16 1000-lb bombs to knock out a field artillery position northeast of Santa Fe.

LAST AERIAL VICTORIES

As previously mentioned, the glory days of aerial combat in the Southwest Pacific had ended with the campaign against Clark Field in late December 1944. The Fifth and Thirteenth Air Forces had claimed more than 100 Japanese aircraft shot down during December alone, and almost as many again would be claimed by the entire FEAF during the remaining eight months of the war.

For the 475th FG the final 16 victories claimed by the group came during two long range B-25 escort missions flown on 28 and 29 March 1945. These engagements provided a fitting end to a remarkable run of success for the group, which had seen it claim 552 aircraft shot down, 61 probably destroyed and 36 damaged in just 19 months of aerial combat. The 49th FG had secured top-scoring honours in the Pacific with 664 kills, but the 475th had achieved its kills at a faster rate than any other unit in-theatre, and had one of the highest average rates of claims for any fighter group in the entire USAAF.

The swan song for the 475th as a fighter group began on 28 March when 24 of its P-38s rendezvoused with B-25s over Capotes Island at 0725 hrs, before proceeding to what was then the Indochina coastline in search of Japanese shipping – landfall was reached at 1045 hrs. The

1Lt Louis DuMontier's P-38L-5 44-25439 *MADU V* sits between missions at Clark Field in early April 1945. He had claimed three kills with an earlier P-38L-1 in November-December 1944 (*Author*)

aircraft approached the mainland at low altitude (between wave-top height and 2000 ft), although the P-38s had reportedly climbed to 10,000 ft by the time numerous enemy fighters were spotted stacked up in loose formations from 18,000 ft down to the water at about 1130 hrs. The latter were circling overhead a Japanese convoy that was sailing just off the Indochina coast.

By the time the engagement ended, nine more enemy fighters had been added to the 475th's tally, including the last victories for Maj John Loisel and Capt Perry Dahl. Loisel was leading the entire 475th FG formation at the head of the 433rd FS, and his after action report details how the dogfight started;

'On 28 March 1945 I was flying in the No 1 position in "Red Flight" in a formation of 20 P-38s. At 1150 hrs, we sighted 12 (unidentified) enemy aircraft milling around between 18,000 ft and the deck. The enemy aircraft were circling over a convoy of vessels just north of Tre Island. I started into a climbing turn, dropped tanks at 7500 ft, began a diving turn and approached two probable "Franks" from astern. The first "Frank" did a sharp left turn as I fired a sighting burst. The second "Frank" continued straight ahead in a slight climb. I gave him a good burst, getting hits immediately on his fuselage and right wing. He burst into flames from the wing-root, did a left turn and headed down steeply, flaming badly. This "Frank" crashed just off the enemy convoy.

Beaming 432nd FS ace Capt Perry Dahl grins with anticipation after being told that his long tour in the Pacific was about to end with his rotation home in June 1945 (*Hoxie*)

'A few minutes later I saw my number four aeroplane attacked by an unidentified enemy aircraft. One aeroplane from another flight drove the enemy aircraft off. 2Lt Wesley Hulett called me and said that his engine was out. I then turned eastward, only to see him diving with another enemy aeroplane on his tail. I scared this one off with a short burst and lost sight of the P-38. I looked around for him after he said both engines were shot out – I couldn't locate him, but told him to head due east and that I would call the Catalina. I then returned to the fight, which had drifted eastward from Tre Island.

'I got in several desultory passes with no observed results. Saw 1Lt C Wacker of the 432nd FS shoot down an enemy aircraft. I left the target area at 1210 hrs, and on my way home I searched the area where 2Lt Hulett had gone down. I also contacted "Cat" and all other aircraft in area, giving them the location of the downed aeroplane (P-38L-5 44-25498). I landed at San Marcelino at 1540 hrs.'

As Maj Loisel noted in his after action report, he had encountered the Ki-84 for the first time, and he gave the fighter high marks. The 11-kill ace recalled his 'desultory' passes long after the war, further commenting that he had a few tricks up his sleeve that did no good against the swift and sleek JAAF fighter that had appeared in the frontline late in the war.

Ace 1Lt Kenneth Hart of the 431st FS emerged from the 28 March encounter as one of the group's high scorers, as his after action report explained;

'I was leading a seven-aircraft flight, with 2Lt T Martin flying in the No 2 position and 1Lt "Bo" Reeves at No 3. At 1155 hrs we reached the target area at 11,000 ft. About ten minutes later we made our first pass on two enemy aircraft, with no results. Shortly after, we were jumped from "seven o'clock", and after a short engagement, I shot one down. I fired a long burst from 30 degrees to 0 degrees as I was pulling up on him from below and he burst into flames. The pilot bailed out northwest of Ninh Hoa at about 1213 hrs.

'A few minutes later we were jumped by four more "Hamps". 1Lt Reeves "split S'ed" and I broke sharply to the left, coming out on a "Hamp's" tail. He skidded and was doing rolls as I fired short bursts at him, knocking large pieces from his tail and hitting his fuselage. There was a flash of flame in the cockpit and the pilot bailed out, the ship crashing at 1217 hrs just south of the first Nip I shot down. I looked over to my right and saw a Nip spinning straight in, which crashed just after, and to the north of where my second Nip had just crashed.

'Upon calling on the radio, I found that the P-38 above it, who had just shot down the Nip, was being flown by 1Lt Reeves. We joined up and gave chase to another Nip to the west. I fired at him out of range, endeavouring to make him turn before he reached cloud cover, but had no success. 1Lt Reeves dove under the cloud as I pulled up above and latched onto the Nip as he came out below. I circled above and watched him shoot it down, the Nip crashing and burning a short distance west of Ben Coi Bay at 1220 hrs. We left the target area shortly afterwards and landed back at home base at 1605 hrs.'

It had been a most satisfying operation for the 475th, except for the loss of 2Lt Wesley Hulett, who was never found – the 433rd FS's Flt Off Charles DeWeese (in P-38L-5 44-25459) was also lost in a separate incident that same day.

The next day, the 475th FG again escorted B-25s to the Indochina coast as the long range anti-shipping offensive continued. Unbeknown to the P-38 pilots involved, their mission on 29 March 1945 would be the last time that the group would encounter Japanese aircraft on the wing. Six 431st FS and four 432nd FS Lightnings arrived in the target area at around 1130 hrs, and moments later 1Lt Laurence LeBaron called out 11 bandits approaching them from the same altitude – 4000 ft – slightly off to their right;

'Our flight made a shallow climbing turn to the right and attacked from "six o'clock". In the initial pass, I fired on a straggler from 200 yards at 30 degrees deflection. However, he saw me at the instant I fired and started a fast turn to the left. I observed several cannon bursts along the right side of the fuselage and on the right wing root. The aeroplane began smoking slightly and slipping down towards the water. My wingman fired several bursts, getting several hits on the wingtip. The aeroplane was seen to hit the water just off shore by 2Lt L Dowler.

'I reversed my turn and swung in behind the main formation in time to see 1Lt Harold Owen hit the other straggler and follow him in a diving turn to the right. As yet, the main enemy force gave no indication of having seen us. I closed rapidly on another wingman from the stern and fired a burst from 150 yards, getting numerous hits on the wings, tail and fuselage, knocking pieces off the wing and tail, and causing him to smoke moderately. Because I overran him, and my wingman, 2Lt John O'Rourke, was attacking another at the same time, the enemy pilot was not seen to crash or bail out. As I overran him, I pulled slightly to the left and gave his leader a burst from astern from about 100 yards. He began smoking violently, with pieces coming off the trailing edge of his wing. He immediately plunged into the water. I also saw another fighter crash in the water about 200 yards to the right at about the same time – the result of 2Lt O'Rourke's attack.

'By this time the rest of the Nips had started to scatter, and as I brought my element around to join 1Lt Owens's element, the remaining Nips slipped in behind us. 1Lt Owen crossed over and broke them up with a head-on pass. In the ensuing dogfight, I saw a Nip make a head-on pass from above on 2Lt Dowler, who pulled up and fired at him from below. The Nip passed over him and crashed into the trees half a mile inland.

'After making several more passes and getting in a few scattered hits, I saw one making for the clouds inland and gave chase. After reversing his turns in several cumulus clouds, he apparently thought he had lost us and straightened out, heading south. I came up from below and directly astern, firing a long burst at about 150 yards. He began coming apart and smoking violently. He crashed and burned at the edge of a small clearing. We circled the area two times, and being low on gas, we returned to base, leaving the target at 1255 hrs and landing at home base at 1530 hrs.'

Although flying with the 431st FS on 29 March, 1Lt John O'Rourke was actually a 432nd FS pilot who had readily offered to fill in for a 'Hades' pilot who had aborted earlier in the mission. And this in-flight swap had later proved to be the main topic of discussion back at Clark Field when the two units argued about whether O'Rourke's 'Zeke 52' kill should have been added to the 431st or 432nd victory tally. It was finally decided to award the victory to the former, giving the 432nd six victories for the mission and a single kill to the 431st.

Victory lists disagree on the exact number, but the group accrued at least 552 verified kills by any tabulation, giving it an impressive average of roughly 22 kills per month from the time it first engaged the enemy in aerial combat.

SUPPORTING THE TROOPS ON THE GROUND

From early April through to the end of June 1945, the 475th FG had to satisfy itself with less glamorous 'ground pounding' missions, rather than the high profile fighter-versus-fighter engagements that had effectively been the group's reason for it being activated in mid 1943. Japanese positions both in the northern Kembu and southern Shimbu areas were gradually worn down with methodical certainty by the FEAF, with small formations of bomb-toting P-38s being used to attack positions stubbornly manned by diehard fanatics rather than ranks of organised troops. Perhaps the most threatening Japanese positions of them all during this period were those defending the Ipo Dam area, as they posed a greater danger to the civilian population in the area than to advancing Allied troops.

April 1945 was one of the worst months for the Japanese war effort, for on the 1st, US forces invaded the island of Okinawa. The subsequent basing of USAAF B-29s here duly exposed the home islands of Kyushu and Honshu to a series of devastating attacks by the long range heavy bombers. Six days later, the mighty battleship *Yamato* was lost in a futile operation against US naval vessels off Okinawa, and on the same day fighter-escorted B-29s began to attack the home islands.

Although heavily committed to the ground war in the Philippines, the 475th was able to alternate tactical strikes with bomber escort and long range ground attack missions against targets along the South-east Asian coast, as well as the island of Formosa. For example, on 1 April the 432nd FS escorted a PBM Mariner that had been sent to patrol the sea around Formosa, and 24 hours later the unit flew an impressive napalm attack mission on the Villa Verde trail, west of Santa Fe. For the latter operation, five P-38s were loaded with 1000-lb general purpose bombs and four armed with napalm. Large fires were started in the target area which caused a US forward air controller to comment over the radio that the group's bombing was the best he had ever witnessed.

The 475th experienced the heaviest mission schedule of its brief operational life during this period, for the short nature of the tactical missions in support of troops on the ground allowed squadrons to fly at least two or three operations a day. And pilots who flew these missions commented that they took great pleasure in attacking railway-related targets in particular. Locomotives were especially gratifying, for when bullets and cannon shells struck the boiler plate of the engine, a spectacular fountain of steam would often whoosh up for hundreds of feet just as the successful P-38 passed overhead.

The 433rd FS got an unexpected crack at railway targets on 8 April when eight of its fighters escorted B-24s that had been sent to bomb an airfield on Formosa. The P-38 pilots had been circling the area for 15 minutes when a locomotive pulling five freight wagons was spotted on the main north-to-south line near the city of Taichu. The train was thoroughly strafed, and by the time the fighters had withdrawn, the engine was hidden in a cloud of steam and its wagons shot to pieces.

Later that same month the 475th gave up its comfortable Clark Field quarters for the dusty and austere conditions at Lingayen. The Mustangs of the 35th FG had been suffering high attrition because of the unrefined surface of the hurriedly built airstrips and runways in the area. Compared

with the P-51, the P-38 had somewhat sturdier landing gear that was better suited to operations from rough surfaces and landing grounds such as those found at Lingayen.

By 19 April the 475th had essentially traded places with the 35th FG, and three days later, the grousing and complaining by the Lightning pilots about the interruption in combat operations ended when the group flew its first missions. For the next few days sorties were flown against ground targets around Baguio until that entire area fell to two American divisions on 26 April. Elsewhere, Japanese forces were found to be entrenching themselves along transport routes into the Cagayan Valley, thus presenting the FEAF's fighter and dive-bomber units with plenty of fixed targets to attack.

This unusual line-up photograph of 475th P-38Ls from all three units was taken late in the war somewhere in the Philippines. It almost certainly shows aircraft sat on the ramp awaiting servicing during a period of intense ground attack operations, when P-38s were literally left queued up wherever space could be found for them as hard-pressed groundcrews struggled to cope with the accelerated sortie rate (*Author*)

The move to Lingayen meant that the 475th was now in a better position from which to attack long-range targets on Formosa and mainland South-east Asia. And even though ground support missions would continue, pilots soon came to appreciate the possibilities offered by this more strategic location.

On 3 May P-38s from the 433rd FS were on a dive-bombing mission to the Bontoc area of the Cordilera Central Mountains when the aircraft of formation leader 1Lt Jerome Hammond was hit by flak. Although one of his engines was ablaze, the pilot managed to force land his P-38 and escape from the wrecked cockpit before it was engulfed by flames. Moments after he had scampered clear of the Lightning, it exploded into a fireball.

1Lt Bob Weary took over the 431st FS's P-38L '135' when Maj Robert Cline left the squadron in June 1945. Weary adopted the name *MISS MANOOKIE* for his aircraft. Note the demon head applied to the radiator housing, this marking appearing on the unit's Lightnings during the move from Leyte to Clark Field in March-April 1945 (*Author*)

For three days Hammond successfully evaded Japanese patrols, and also his own comrades when P-38s dive-bombed a nearby target, until he was found by friendly Filipino partisans. He was then taken to an Allied camp, where he received food, clothes and treatment for the burns he had received during the crash. Eager to help him out, the Filipinos had guided Hammond back to Lingayen by 19 May, where he rejoined his comrades.

He left the Pacific for good in July when he was rotated back home to Wichita, in Kansas.

While Jerome Hammond was making his way back through enemy lines, the drive toward the Ipo Dam was progressing at great speed. The 475th was heavily involved in this offensive, flying numerous missions against enemy positions in the immediate target area between 17 and 26 May. By this time the dreaded napalm was really beginning to have an effect on the morale of Japanese troops, and the latter wilted in the face of continual attacks to the point where the commander of the US Army's 43rd Division sent the 475th a commendation for its part in making the sweep through the area so effortless.

June 1945 saw the end of all organised resistance by the Japanese in northern Luzon, and with enemy forces in the south having been all but defeated, there was little for the FEAF's tactical units to do except strike at occasional targets in the Aparri region of northern Luzon. By month-end the Philippines had been declared secure, and only occasional mopping up missions were now being flown. On 18 June the 475th would commence long range napalm missions with a strike on Kari, in southwestern Formosa.

1Lt Joe Forster's P-38L-5 44-25132 *FLORIDA CRACKER* is seen with the ace's full kill tally below the cockpit. The aircraft was subsequently adorned with radiating sight angle lines on the wing immediately outboard of the cockpit, as Forster realised that his job would be exclusively ground attack after he returned from his gunnery course in July 1945 (*Author*)

TOUR ROTATION

Gen Douglas MacArthur had officially declared the Philippines secure on 26 June 1945, thus tacitly approving a general rotation back home for all FEAF personnel. And although MacArthur never put much stock in pampering his troops, giving little thought to sparing soldiers from the demands of combat, his views were not shared by Lt Gen Kenney of the FEAF. Indeed, the latter had gone out of his way to protect his aircrew, believing that they could only be kept sharp in combat if tour limits were rigorously adhered to.

In practice, this meant that a fighter pilot in the Fifth Air Force could typically expect to be eligible for rotation after about 300 hours in combat or about 15 months on tour, unless he accepted a position of advanced responsibility such as operations officer or squadron commander.

Aces Perry Dahl and Joe Forster had both joined the 475th FG's 432nd FS in late October 1943. Destined to be aces by the end of 1944, they had remained in-theatre until mid 1945. The only break from frontline flying that Dahl had experienced during this period came in November-December 1944, when he evaded capture for a month in the Philippines after being forced down following a mid-air collision. Forster had spent several months in the US in early 1945 attending a gunnery class, but was back in the Philippines by July – just after Dahl had rotated home in late June. Both men had enjoyed great success with the 432nd FS, claiming nine confirmed kills apiece and surviving numerous combat missions.

Although Dahl had spent an impressive 21 months in-theatre (he had agreed to accept the post of operations officer for the 432nd FS), this did not come close to the three years of service Lt Col John Loisel gave to the 475th FG. He had joined the group upon its formation in July 1943 after being given a six-month extension to his tour following nine months in combat with the 36th FS/8th FG. Loisel progressed through the ranks within the 475th, being operations officer and then CO of the 432nd FS in 1943-44, after whch he became group operations officer when Maj McGuire was killed in January 1945. By then an 11-victory ace, he was finally made commander of the 475th FG when veteran CO Col MacDonald was sent home in July 1945.

Another pilot who completed an extended spell in the frontline was five-kill ace 1Lt Marion Kirby, who agreed to extend for six months when he was assigned to the 431st FS in July 1943. He had already spent close to 12 months in New Guinea with the 80th FS/8th FG by the time he transferred to the 475th, and was glad to rotate home in December 1943 after completing some 126 combat missions.

Although virtually all fighter pilots assigned to the 475th FG were keen to see action, Lt Col John Loisel told the author that nobody ever turned down a trip home when orders terminating a tour were received.

For enlisted groundcrew, tours tended to last a lot longer. One individual who took this to an extreme was MSgt Clay V Cockerill, who had joined the 475th in Australia in July 1943 and remained with the group until he was rotated home exactly two years later. He had managed to successfully resist

432nd FS groundcrews unpack a brand new P-38L-5 late in the war. This photograph was almost certainly taken in the Philippines judging by the serial number applied on the fighter's nose – a late war practice (Hoxie)

being sent home until he fell under the provisions of the 'over 40 years of age' ruling.

Just prior to Cockerill being sent home, he participated in a group-wide gathering on 20 June 1945 at Lingayen which saw the 475th finally receive its three Distinguished Unit Citations. The first of these had been awarded to the unit as long ago as August 1943 following its impressive introduction into battle over Wewak on the 18th and 21st of that month, when its pilots not only protected the bombers, but also claimed many Japanese aircraft shot down.

The second citation followed the group's gallant fight over Oro Bay on 15 and 17 October 1943, when ground personnel were able to witness for themselves the clashes in which the P-38s disrupted Japanese attacks and claimed many more enemy aircraft destroyed.

1Lt John Tilley's P-38L-5 *Bette Ann* was also marked with his full complement of five victory flags when this photograph was taken on Luzon in 1945 (*Author*)

The third award came in the wake of the whirlwind of action in which many more Japanese aircraft were shot down between 25 October and 25 December 1944 during the climactic air battles over the Philippines in the initial stages of the invasion. In March 1946 the group received yet another honour when Maj Thomas Buchanan McGuire was posthumously awarded the Congressional Medal of Honor. Maj Richard Ira Bong's service with the 475th in December 1944 had also been mentioned in the citation which accompanied his Medal of Honor, presented to the American ace of aces that same month.

FINAL COMBAT

Following almost 24 months of near constant action, July 1945 at last provided the 475th FG's hard-pressed groundcrews with a little respite from having to provide serviceable P-38s for the two to three missions that the group had typically been flying on a near-daily basis since mid 1943. With a lack of targets to be serviced, groundcrews now had seemingly unlimited time for maintenance and the replenishment of supplies. They were even able to take a break from the flightline and parade in front of Brig Gen Freddie Smith, who had travelled to Lingayen Gulf in order to present 151 decorations to the 75 pilots then serving with the group. This would be the last such presentation conducted by the 475th in wartime.

Combat operations had not entirely stopped, however, for the group was still occasionally attacking ragged pockets of resistance stubbornly and defiantly posed by exhausted Japanese forces, mainly in the extreme northern part of Luzon. By late July even these missions had tailed off, so the 49th and 475th FGs were relieved of combat duty on the 23rd of the month in preparation for their impending move to bases in the Japanese home islands area.

Forty-eight hours earlier, the latter groups' three squadrons had flown what would prove to be their last combat missions of the war. The 431st would undertake mission number 1-1008, the 432nd would send eight P-38s on a fire-bombing attack northwest of Kiangan for mission number 2-907 and the 433rd would perform a convoy cover patrol for mission number 3-1047. All subsequent sorties from Lingayen over the next five days would be either training or operational administrative flights. Even these ceased on 26 July, when the group commenced packing up in preparation for movement closer to Japan itself.

Personnel from the 431st FS were loaded aboard LST 793, the 432nd FS boarded LST 752 and the 433rd FS embarked in LST 1014. All three vessels left Lingayen Gulf on the morning of 27 July, and they reached the naval base in Subic Bay, in the Philippines, the next day. By 1 August the group was sailing again, with the HQ aboard LST 752 and other elements of the 431st aboard cramped LSMs which accompanied the convoy.

On 6 August the group arrived in convoy off Okinawa, and the 432nd FS's operational diarist recorded this event, totally unaware of the significance of a bombing mission that had taken place that same morning – the atomic bomb 'Little Boy' had been dropped on Hiroshima;

'Land was sighted this morning – Okinawa. Our LST dropped anchor in Yonobura Harbour at 1130 hrs. Next to Naha, this is the second most important harbour on the island. The amount of shipping in Yonobura surpassed everything we had laid eyes on before. Almost every conceivable type of vessel and craft used by the Navy and Merchant Marine were either anchored or seen plying the waters between ship and shore. Our LST was anchored close enough off shore for us to be able to observe a few of the numerous strips reputed to be on Okinawa, and some of us had the opportunity of viewing for the first time the much vaunted "battleship of the air" – the B-29.

'We remained in Yonobura Harbour, awaiting our turn to disgorge our load on the beach at Ie Shima, which is about a two-and-a-half hour trip from here. Ie Shima has facilities for unloading only four or five LSTs at a time, and the arrival of our convoy is overtaxing those facilities. It will probably be four or five days before our turn to unload comes up.'

The first air raid alert for the 475th since 5 March in the Philippines was heard in the early morning hours of 7 August. Two more air raids later that day caused more anxiety, since news of the atomic bombing had drawn speculation that the war might be coming to a sudden end. A second atomic bomb dropped on Nagasaki, and the Soviet Union's declaration of war on Japan on the 9th, presaged the general collapse of Japanese will.

Ie Shima itself was described by a 475th officer as 'a combination of Biak and Leyte. The roads, which were all constructed of coral, were marvels of engineering skill, but our camp area was a muddy morass that

Aircraft of the 432nd FS are lined up ready for inspection in late July 1945. P-38L-5 44-25600 *BLOOD AND GUTS III* of ten-kill ace, and squadron CO, Capt Elliott Summer is parked closest to the camera (*Author*)

had to be covered with coral before it could become even halfway livable'. When the group finally disembarked on 12 August, everybody was immediately pressed into service to make the camp come to life in record time.

Capt Elliott Summer had been interim commander of the 432nd FS until 28 July 1945, when he was rotated home and Maj Dean Dutrack took over the unit just as it began its move to Ie Shima. Maj Ed Weaver, who had been part of the fateful 'Daddy Special' flight on 7 January over Negros Island, was in command of the 431st FS at war's end, while 433rd FS records have the signature of veteran group pilot Capt William Haning as commander during the July-August 1945 period.

For the last few months of operations, the 475th dropped more than 1400 tons of high explosives and 1600+ gallons of napalm at a time when few missions involved more than eight P-38s. As these figures show, the group had been highly active in its role supporting Allied ground forces. And whether the latter recognised the twin-boomed aeroplanes over their heads or not, the troops on Luzon and Leyte owed some gratitude to the persistent skill of the 475th pilots who bombed and strafed determined, if ragged, Japanese troops barring the way to clearing the islands.

Between August 1943 and the end of March 1945, the 475th's 552 aerial victories had cost it 80 P-38s lost in combat and 75 pilots killed in action. 1Lt William Hasty of the 433rd FS, who had been downed in June 1944 and captured on the Vogelkop peninsula, became the only 475th prisoner of war to be repatriated after VJ-Day.

POSTWAR POSTSCRIPT

Members of the 475th FG were satisfied to see two white 'Betty' bombers with their distinctive green crosses on their fuselage and wings land at Mocha strip on Ie Shima at around noon on 19 August 1945. Brig Gen Freddie Smith of V Fighter Command was on hand to greet the grim-faced Japanese delegation flown in aboard the aircraft, and he saw them off again aboard a C-54 some 90 minutes later. They would fly on to Manila, where the last details of the new peace were to be negotiated before the 2 September 1945 ceremony that was staged aboard the battleship USS *Missouri* officially brought World War 2 to an end.

These 431st FS P-38L-5s are being inspected either in South Korea or Japan soon after the end of the Pacific War (Author)

Throughout the war in the Southwest Pacific, V Fighter Command had been a painful thorn in the side of the Japanese, and the 475th had been the barb end of that thorn for much of the time. As previously mentioned, final figures of enemy aircraft shot down grant the 49th FG top spot with 664 confirmed claims, followed by the 475th with 552, the 8th with 453, the 35th with 387 and the 348th with 349. The tactically-assigned 58th FG managed 14 kills while flying under conditions that were not conducive to aerial combat.

The first post-war move for the 475th was to Kimpo, in South Korea, in September 1945. Those crews who had endured the last operations of the Pacific War now had to cope with the usual level of neglect associated with the reduction in the size of armed forces after any large-scale conflict. To make matters worse, the group was subjected to freezing winter weather in South Korea in 1945-46. Fortunately, the ravaged Japanese wartime economy came to the rescue when surplus fur-lined flying suits and barracks heaters were procured from the 475th's former adversaries.

In 1946 the group converted to the P-51 Mustang in an action that would have been anathema to the wartime veterans who had sworn by their P-38s. Finally, in 1948, the 475th moved to Itazuke and then Ashiya, both in Japan, before being deactivated in April, 1949. The group remained dormant until mid 1953, when the 431st was activated within the 7272nd Flying Training Wing. Inadvertently, one of the first experiences the author had had with the 475th was when he observed the F-89s of the 432nd Fighter-Interceptor Squadron (FIS), based at Minneapolis/St Paul International Airport, flying over his teenaged head in the mid-1950s!

The 431st FIS converted to F-86D Sabres in the mid 1950s, after which it operated from Wheelus air base, in Libya, before the squadron moved to Zaragosa, in Spain, in 1958. There, it converted to the F-102 Delta Dart in 1960, and the squadron was still operating the type when it was transferred to Southeast Asia in the mid-1960s. At about the same time, the 433rd FS was reactivated and issued with F-4C Phantom IIs, prior to being assigned to the 9th Tactical Fighter Wing. During the Vietnam conflict, pilots assigned to the 433rd FIS scored a number of aerial victories, thus raising its historical tally to more than 130 enemy aircraft shot down.

As of late 2006, it is still possible to visit with some of the personalities who actually lived the colourful history of the 'Satan's Angels', as the veterans of the group are pleased to call themselves. Col John Loisel still maintains a military bearing that constantly breaks down into cheery friendliness when he talks about those days. Perry Dahl is much the same, making me wonder who gave him the nickname 'Pee Wee' whenever I shake his hand and feel the viselike grip of his enduring arm muscle. Joe Forster is still a lean and efficient looking individual, and it is not hard to imagine the venerable fighter pilot guiding his battle-damaged P-38 the 800+ miles from Borneo back to northern New Guinea.

Many of the others are gone, of course. Col MacDonald was the very spirit of the group, and it is hard to believe that his gently dominating presence is gone. Fred Champlin was a quiet chap who remained a standard of 'Satan's Angels'' valour and determination until he slowly succumbed some years ago. But we can imagine them all, from the charismatic Tom McGuire to the line mechanics glowing with fierce pride in their job of work that championed our cause in a terrible and unfortunate war.

APPENDICES

APPENDIX 1

VICTORIES SCORED BY THE 475th FG

Headquarters	43
431st Fighter Squadron	221
432nd Fighter Squadron	167
433rd Fighter Squadron	121
Total	**552**

APPENDIX 2

475th FIGHTER GROUP FIGHTER ACES

Maj Thomas B McGuire (431st FS and HQ)	38†	Capt Billy M Gresham (432nd FS)	6†
Col Charles H MacDonald (HQ)	27	Capt James C Ince (432nd FS)	6(2)
Capt Daniel T Roberts (432nd and 433rd FSs)	14(4)†	Capt Paul W Lucas (432nd FS)	6†
Capt Francis Lent (431st FS)	11†	2Lt John C Smith (433rd FS)	6†
Lt Col John S Loisel (432nd FS and HQ)	11	Capt Horace B Reeves (431st FS)	6
Capt Elliot Summer (432nd FS)	10	Capt Joseph A McKeon (433rd FS)	6(2)
Capt Fredric F Champlin (431st FS)	9	Capt Arthur E Wenige (431st FS)	6(1)
Capt Perry J Dahl (432nd FS)	9	Capt Harry W Brown (431st FS)	6(2)
Capt Joseph M Forster (432nd FS)	9	Capt Henry L Condon (432nd FS)	5†
Lt Col Meryl M Smith (HQ)	9†	Capt Grover D Gholson (432nd FS)	5(1)
1Lt David W Allen (431st FS)	8(2)	1Lt Marion F Kirby (431st FS)	5
Capt Frederick A Harris (432nd FS)	8†	1Lt Lowell C Lutton (431st FS)	5†
Capt Kenneth F Hart (431st FS)	8	Capt Jack C Mankin (431st FS)	5(1)
1Lt Zach W Dean (432nd FS)	7	1Lt Frank H Monk (431st FS)	5
1Lt Vincent T Elliott (431st FS)	7	Capt Paul V Morriss (431st FS)	5
Capt Jack A Fisk (433rd FS)	7	Maj Franklin A Nichols (431st FS)	5(4)
Capt Verl A Jett (431st FS)	7(1)	Capt John A Tilley (431st FS)	5
Maj Warren R Lewis (431st and 433rd FSs)	7		
Capt John E Purdy (433rd FS)	7		
Maj Calvin C Wire (433rd FS)	7	() – indicates victories scored with other units	
1Lt Edward J Czarnecki (431st FS)	6	† – killed in action/flying accident	

APPENDIX 3

475th FIGHTER GROUP CASUALTIES

Name	Unit	Date	Remarks
Lt Richard E Dotson	431st	5 July 1943	killed in training crash
Lt Andrew K Duke	431st	9 August 1943	killed in flying accident
Lt Ralph E Schmidt	431st	18 August 1943	killed in action
Lt Allen Camp	432nd	20 August 1943	killed in flying accident
Lt Richard Ryrholm	432nd	4 September 1943	missing in action (later changed to killed in action)
Lt Chester D Phillips	432nd	8 September 1943	missing in action
Lt John C Knox	431st	13 September 1943	killed in action
Lt Noel R Lundy	432nd	13 September 1943	declared killed in action on 18 January 1944
Lt Donald Garrison	432nd	22 September 1943	killed in action
Lt Raymond Corrigan	433rd	24 September 1943	killed in action
Lt Kenneth D Kirshner	433rd	24 September 1943	PoW, and later died in captivity
Lt Virgil F Hagan	433rd	17 October 1943	killed in action
? Edward Hedrick	431st	17 October 1943	killed in action
Lt Edward Czarnecki	431st	23 October 1943	shot down and rescued, but died in 1976 after years of illness with tropical disease contracted in North Borneo
Lt Christopher Bartlett	432nd	29 October 1943	shot down and hidden by local villagers until Japanese informed of his position by German missionary and captured, then executed
Capt Fredrick A Harris	432nd	31 October 1943	killed in flying accident
Lt Kenneth M Richardson	431st	2 November 1943	killed in action
Lt Lowell C Lutton	431st	2 November 1943	killed in action
Lt Leo M Mayo	432nd	2 November 1943	missing in action (later changed to killed in action)
Lt Donald Y King	433rd	2 November 1943	killed in action
Lt Paul Smith	431st	8 November 1943	missing in action
Lt John Smith	433rd	9 November 1943	killed in action
Capt Daniel T Roberts	433rd	9 November 1943	killed in action
Lt Dale O Meyer	433rd	9 November 1943	killed in action
Lt Theodore Fostakowski	431st	15 November 1943	killed in flying accident
Lt Robert J Smith	431st	16 November 1943	missing in action
Lt Ormand E Powell	431st	28 December 1943	missing in action
Lt John E Fogarty	432nd	13 January 1944	killed in flying accident
Lt Richard Hancock	433rd	16 January 1944	missing in action (body subsequently recovered and interred in Fort Bonifacio cemetery in the Philippines)
Lt William Ritter	432nd	18 January 1944	PoW, then executed
Lt John R Weldon	431st	18 January 1944	missing in action
Lt Joseph A Robertson	431st	18 January 1944	killed in action
Lt McCleod Jones	431st	21 January 1944	posted missing whilst co-pilot of B-25 on detached service
Lt Martin J Hawthorne	431st	22 January 1944	killed in flying accident
Lt Carl A Danforth	433rd	23 January 1944	missing in action
Lt Donald D Revenaugh	433rd	23 January 1944	missing in action
Lt Wood D Clodfelter	431st	14 February 1944	killed in flying accident
Lt Harold Howard	432nd	29 February 1944	killed in flying accident
Lt Robert P Donald	431st	31 March 1944	killed in action
Flt Off Joe B Barton	432nd	3 April 1944	killed in action
Lt Jack F Luddington	431st	16 April 1944	missing in action

Name	Unit	Date	Remarks
Lt Milton A MacDonald	431st	16 April 1944	missing in action
Lt Robert L Hubner	432nd	16 April 1944	missing in action
Lt Louis L Longman	433rd	16 April 1944	missing in action
Lt Austin K Neely	433rd	16 April 1944	missing in action
Lt Louis M Yarbrough	433rd	16 April 1944	missing in action
Lt Troy L Martin	432nd	11 June 1944	killed in flying accident
Lt Howard V Stiles	433rd	16 June 1944	missing in action
Lt Robert L Crosswait	431st	30 June 1944	missing in action
Lt William A Elliot	432nd	28 July 1944	missing in action
Capt William S O'Brien	431st	4 August 1944	killed in action
Lt Nathaniel V Landen	431st	19 September 1944	killed in action
Lt Walter W Weisfus	432nd	24 September 1944	killed in flying accident (in P-39)
Lt Charles H Joseph	433rd	1 October 1944	killed in flying accident
Capt Billy M Gresham	432nd	2 October 1944	killed in flying accident
Lt Donald W Patterson	431st	13 October 1944	killed in flying accident
Lt Arnold R Neilson	431st	2 November 1944	killed in flying accident
Lt Grady M Laseter	432nd	10 November 1944	killed in action
Lt Erland J Varland	431st	24 November 1944	missing in action
Lt Morton B Ryerson	433rd	6 December 1944	killed in action
Lt Col Meryl M Smith	HQ	7 December 1944	killed in action
Lt Robert H Koeck	431st	25 December 1944	killed in action
Lt Enrique Provencio	431st	25 December 1944	killed in action
Lt Clifford L Ettien	433rd	31 December 1944	killed in action
Capt Henry L Condon II	432nd	2 January 1945	killed in action
Maj Thomas B McGuire	431st	7 January 1945	killed in action
Maj Jack B Rittmayer	431st	7 January 1945	killed in action
Capt Paul W Lucas	432nd	16 January 1945	killed in action
Lt Robert Patterson	431st	29 January 1945	missing in action
Flt Off Charles C Nacke	432nd	29 January 1945	missing in action
Lt Arthur J Schmidt	431st	15 February 1945	missing in action
Flt Off Charles R DeWeese	433rd	28 March 1945	killed in action
Lt Wesley J Hulett	433rd	28 March 1945	killed in action
Lt Laverne P Busch	433rd	2 April 1945	recovered, but died from injuries on 5 April 1945
Lt Reed L Pietscher	432nd	15 April 1945	killed in action
Lt Millard R Sherman	431st	30 May 1945	killed in action
Lt Alvin G Roth	431st	18 June 1945	killed in action
Lt Edward Carley	431st	18 June 1945	killed in action
Lt Herbert S Finney	431st	21 June 1945	killed in flying accident
Lt Charles C Zarling	433rd	8 July 1945	killed in flying accident
Capt George W Smith	HQ	11 July 1945	killed in flying accident

Also, on 22 February 1945 a runaway P-47 careered into the 433rd FS flightline, killing crew chiefs SSgt Charles Huff, Sgt Edward J Hamilton and Cpl William E Maddock

COLOUR PLATES

1

P-38F/G (serial unknown) of 1Lt Charles Grice, 433rd FS, Port Moresby and Dobodura, August 1943

A number of P-38F/Gs were acquired by the newly-formed 475th FG from operational units in-theatre upon the group's arrival in New Guinea in August 1943. This otherwise unidentified Lightning was obtained from the 39th FS/35th FG, hence its blue spinners and sharksmouth on the engine nacelles. According to most 475th FG veterans, these hand-me-down P-38s were primarily used for training, although a handful of F/G-models appear to have remained operational with the group until early 1944. 1Lt Charles Grice claimed four kills in late 1943, although whether he claimed any in this machine remains unknown.

2

P-38H-5 42-66750 of 2Lt Arthur G Peregoy, 432nd FS, Dobodura, October 1943

Although assigned to 2Lt Art Peregoy, this aircraft was used by early group ace 2Lt Billy Gresham to claim his first kill (almost certainly a Ki-45) on 21 August 1943. Peregoy claimed the first of his two victories with 42-66750 during the 'Bloody Tuesday' clash over Rabaul on 2 November 1943, when he downed a Zero. This aircraft was eventually replaced by a P-38J during the early months of 1944.

3

P-38H-5 42-66827 of 1Lt Marion F Kirby, 431st FS, Dobodura, October 1943

1Lt Marion Kirby began flying this P-38 as his regular mount in October 1943, and he used it to score his final victories over Rabaul during 'Bloody Tuesday'. The two 'Zekes' that Kirby claimed on this day took his overall tally of kills to exactly five destroyed, thus giving him ace status. Photographs of this aircraft suggest that it had dark blue spinner tips, rather than the standard solid red.

4

P-38H-5 42-66742 of Capt Verl E Jett, 431st FS, Dobodura, November 1943

This was Capt Verl Jett's regular mount when he assumed command of the 431st FS on 22 November 1943. Already a five-kill ace by then, he had the squadron commander's number ('110') applied to the nose and tail booms of his aircraft, and added the single boom command stripe. Jett claimed two Ki-43s destroyed with this aircraft near Wewak on 18 August 1943, and possibly 'made ace' in the fighter on 13 September when he downed a Ki-45 again near Wewak. Fellow ace Capt Harry Brown scored his sixth, and last, kill in 42-66742 when he destroyed a 'Zeke' near Rabaul on 24 October 1943.

5

P-38H-5 42-66843 of 2Lt Calvin C Wire, 433rd FS, Dobodura, September 1943

2Lt Calvin Wire used this P-38 to score his second and third victories on 26 September 1943, the future seven-kill ace downing two 'Oscars' over Wewak. He had taken charge of this near-new P-38 just days prior to claiming these victories, and he quickly developed a fondness for the aeroplane. Therefore, Wire was very irate with his crew chief when he allowed Maj MacDonald to commandeer 42-66843 on 15 October 1943. The future group CO dived headlong into a formation of Japanese dive-bombers literally as he took off in Wire's fighter, claiming two 'Vals' destroyed before he was himself badly shot up by Zeros over Oro Bay. MacDonald nursed the P-38 back to Dobodura and belly-landed it on the runway. The fighter was duly sent off to a service squadron to be repaired.

6

P-38H-1 42-66550 of 2Lt Francis J Lent, 431st FS, Dobodura, November 1943

2Lt Frank Lent paired up with 1Lt Tom McGuire soon after the 475th FG arrived in New Guinea, and both pilots quickly became aces. Lent scored the first nine of his eleven victories in the long-lived 42-66550, claiming these kills between 18 August and 16 December 1943. The aircraft enjoyed a remarkably trouble-free life until it was replaced by P-38J-15 42-104032 in early 1944.

7

P-38H-5 (serial unknown) of 1Lt Elliot Summer, 432nd FS, Dobodura, December 1943

Elliot Summer was a typical New Englander with a baritone Yankee brogue who apparently showed little preference for any single Lightning, although he called this one (possibly P-38H-1 42-66541) his own and had marked it to his liking by December 1943. The fighter featured six victory symbols for Summer's kills between 21 August and 22 December 1943. Although he was rather reticent about his wartime experiences when interviewed by the author many years later, it can be safely assumed that Summer ran through P-38s quickly considering that this one was the third that he had used in combat by December 1943.

8

P-38J-10 42-67597 of 1Lt Fredric F Champlin, 431st FS, Dobodura, January 1944

42-67597 was one of the first J-models to reach the 475th FG in early 1944, and Fred Champlin felt that it was a 'bad luck' aircraft. According to the nine-kill ace, it had a history of minor mechanical problems which ensured that its pilot would either abort the mission or be obliged to take up a substitute aircraft. Legend has it that the number '113' was never assigned to another Lightning in the 431st again after 42-67597. Champlin only used the fighter for a very short time in early 1944, before passing it on to a service squadron on 15 February. He flew P-38s bearing the number '112' for the rest of his combat tour.

9

P-38J-5 42-67290 of 1Lt Ferdinand E Hanson, 432nd FS, Dobodura, January 1944

Another early-build J-model P-38, 42-67290 carried Disney-inspired nose art in the form of 'Ferdinand the Bull' because the character shared the same unusual first name as the pilot of this aircraft, 1Lt Ferdinand Hanson. The aircraft was also adorned with a small clover leaf on its nose beneath the guns (applied on a freshly repainted area of the forward fuselage), this emblem being the symbol of the 432nd FS. His earlier P-38H-1 (42-66632), which had been replaced with this aircraft on 13 December 1943, also featured the bull motif, and it was probably this machine that Hanson used to score a probable on 2 November.

10

P-38J-15 42-104035 of Maj Warren R Lewis, 433rd FS, Biak, June 1944

As CO of the 433rd FS, Maj Lewis was assigned one of the first natural metal P-38s to be issued to his unit in late January 1944. He may well have used this aircraft to 'make ace' on 3 April 1944, when he downed an 'Oscar' over Hollandia. Lewis' subsequent claims on 16 and 19 May (another 'Oscar' and a 'Pete' seaplane), which took his final tally to seven kills, could also have been scored in this machine, as it served with the unit until September 1944.

11

P-38H-1 42-66504 of 2Lt Perry J Dahl, 432nd FS, Dobodura, January 1944

Dahl was variously dubbed 'Pee Wee' and 'Lucky', both for his diminutive size and for his propensity to escape close calls in combat. This aircraft was issued to Dahl soon after he joined the 432nd FS on 26 October 1943, and he duly named it *23 SKIDOO* after an expession that was popular in the 'Roaring Twenties'. He also had an inebriated, 'red-nosed', Tomahawk-wielding Indian warrior painted onto the nose of his P-38. Proving his ability as a fighter pilot, Dahl used the aircraft to destroy an 'Oscar' on his very first encounter with the enemy during the 9 November 1943 mission to Alexishafen. According to Dahl, he flew this machine well into January 1944.

12

P-38J-15 (serial unknown) of Maj Thomas B McGuire, 431st FS, Biak, late July 1944

Despite being well photographed, the exact identity of *"Pudgy IV"* remains uncertain. Accepted by McGuire in the summer of 1944 (in July or August) probably on Biak Island, this aircraft was flown by the ace for about three months. It is quite possible that McGuire claimed no kills with the fighter, as his only victories during this period came during his solitary sortie to Balikpapan with the 49th FG on 14 October 1944, when he was almost certainly required to use one of its machines. McGuire was notorious for flying his P-38s hard, thus shortening their lifespan of five or six months to just three or four. He flew his second Pudgy (P-38H-5 42-66817) from September 1943 to January 1944, and the third (serial unknown) from February to July, making it the longest lived of all his Lightnings. Note that this aircraft wears command stripes, as McGuire was CO of the 431st FS at this time.

13

P-38J-15 42-104319 of Capt Herbert Cochran, 433rd FS, Biak, July 1944

Capt Herbert Cochran was a native of Decatur, Illinois, hence the name he gave to his P-38. It is possible that this was the aircraft that he was flying when he was forced to ditch off Biak in July 1944.

14

P-38J-15 42-104308 of 1Lt Carroll J Anderson, 433rd FS, Biak, July 1944

1Lt Carroll Anderson probably took charge of this P-38J-15

sometime between April and June 1944. He and his crew chief, TSgt Ruiz, decided to give the natural metal fighter an elaborate blue paint scheme which included white-bordered diagonal wing stripes. However, this striking decoration did not last long before someone in higher authority ordered that the fighter wear a more orthodox scheme in conformity with squadron practice. Anderson used the P-38 until he rotated home at year-end. It carried the name *Margaret* on its right gun bay door.

15

P-38J-15 42-104024 of Col Charles H MacDonald, 475th HQ, Biak, July 1944

The group commander was senior enough in rank to take the pick of any new aircraft coming into the group, and this particular P-38 was the first Lightning selected by Lt Col MacDonald after he assumed command of the 475th FG on 26 November 1943. It was actually the second P-38 (a P-47 in the 340th FS/348th FG had actually been the first aircraft to don the name) to be dubbed *PUTT PUTT MARU* by MacDonald, and it became his mount in late January 1944. He had ten kills to his name when he began flying 42-104024, and claimed three more with this aircraft prior to it being written off in a flying accident in August 1944.

16

P-38L-5 44-25432 of 1Lt Joseph M Forster, 433rd FS, Dulag, late December 1944

Joe Forster used squadron number '149' for much of his long tour with the 433rd FS, and enjoyed great success with the L-model P-38 in the final months of 1944. Aside from claiming his final six victories with various L-1s between October and December, he also used one to set an unofficial record for the longest single-engined flight in a Lightning when he was forced to fly 850 miles from Balikpapan to Biak on his own in a battle-damaged aircraft on 14 October 1944. Forster took charge of this L-5 soon after he had claimed his final kill on Christmas Day 1944. Note the angle sighting lines on the fuselage immediately below the cockpit, these markings being used by the pilot to align his dive-bombing runs on ground targets. This aircraft remained assigned to Forster until he returned to the USA to attend a gunnery course in March 1945.

17

P-38L-1 44-24155 of Maj Thomas B McGuire, 431st FS, Dulag, early November 1944

McGuire's most successful P-38 was undoubtedly *PUDGY (V)*, alias 44-24155, which he flew from late October through to early January 1945, when the Lightning was removed from the frontline and sent to a servicing unit for overhaul. By then McGuire had claimed at least 14 kills with it, taking his final tally to 38 victories. It is depicted here after he had claimed his first success (a Ki-44 'Tojo') with the fighter on 1 November 1944. *PUDGY (V)* was sat at Dulag awaiting despatch to a servicing unit when McGuire sortied for the last time (in 431st FS P-38L-1 44-24845) on 7 January 1945.

18

P-38L-5 44-25930 of 1Lt John E Purdy, 433rd FS, Dulag, December 1944

1Lt John Purdy was issued with this P-38L after losing his previous *LIZZIE* in a crash-landing on 11 December 1944 – the mission he 'made ace' on. He probably used *LIZZIE V* to score his last two kills (both A6M5 Zeros) on 17 December near Mindoro Island. Purdy confirmed to the author that this aircraft was lost in a crash-landing on 9 January 1945.

19

P-38J-15 42-104494 of Capt Chase Brenizer, 433rd FS, Dulag, December 1944

Capt Chase Brenizer was ostensibly a ladies' man, for his aircraft was marked up with seven female names within an inverted spade symbol painted onto the right side of the gondola. However, there is speculation amongst surviving 433rd FS groundcrew that these names referred to the women in the lives of all air- and groundcrew assigned to the fighter. Brenizer used this P-38 to score his second, and final, kill over the Philippines on 7 December 1944.

20

P-38H-5 42-66836 of Maj Franklin A Nichols, 431st FS, Dobodura, October 1943

This aircraft was the second Lightning assigned to 431st FS CO Maj Frank Nichols in New Guinea, the fighter replacing P-38H-1 42-66540 in late September. It did not last long in the frontline, however, for on 17 October 1Lt Tom McGuire used it to shoot down three 'Zekes' over Oro Bay before he himself fell victim to the Japanese fighters.

21

P-38L-5 44-25643 of Col Charles H MacDonald, Dulag, January 1945

The fourth of MacDonald's *PUTT PUTT MARUs*, this aircraft had the shortest service life of them all – about three weeks, between 3 and 27 January 1945 – and failed to claim a single kill. On the 27th, deputy group CO Maj John Loisel had stopped the fighter at the end of Dulag strip No 1 following the completion of a mission, and was observing the rest of his flight landing on the rainy runway, when the 432nd FS's Lt Arnold Larsen landed 'hot and flat' in P-38L-1 44-23921. The latter skidded straight into the stationary Loisel, and both fighters had to be despatched to the 10th Service Squadron for repairs to be effected. 44-25643 was later issued to the 8th FG's 80th FS.

22

P-38L-5 44-26177 of 1Lt Thomas E Martin, Clark Field, April 1945

1Lt Tom 'Pepper' Martin accounted for three enemy aircraft (a Zero, a 'Rufe' floatplane fighter and a 'Hamp') between 25 December 1944 and 28 March 1945, all of them were probably scored in this P-38L. The devil's head motif on the boom radiator was applied during April 1945, when the marking came into vogue in the 431st FS.

23

P-38L-1 44-23987 of the 433rd FS, Clark Field, April 1945

2Lt Henry Toll flew a P-38 ('142') which he christened *Strictly Laffs!!* in the 432nd FS in 1944-45, and this example, serving with the 433rd FS, had the same nickname. Notes scribbled onto the back of a photograph featuring this aircraft suggest that 1Lt Jack Fisk may have occasionally flown this P-38, as well as his assigned '191'.

24

P-38L-5 44-26404 of 1Lt Thomas F Fenton, Clark Field, April 1945

This aircraft had some of the largest nose art seen on any 475th FG P-38 in the latter stages of the Pacific War. Its pilot, 1Lt Floyd Fenton, did not join the 431st FS until January 1945, and was still assigned to the squadron come VJ-Day.

25

P-38L-5 44-25471 of Col Charles H MacDonald, 475th FG HQ, Lingayen, July 1945

The fifth, and final, *PUTT PUTT MARU*, this aircraft accounted for Col MacDonald's last victory when he used it to down a 'Topsy' transport aircraft off the coast of Indochina on 13 February 1945. Following MacDonald's rotation home in July, Lt Col John Loisel took over as CO of the group and replaced 44-25471 with his own P-38L.

26

P-38L-5 44-25878 of 1Lt Thomas M Oxford, 431st FS, Lingayen, April 1945

1Lt Tom Oxford flew this P-38 during the final months of the Pacific War. The first *Doots* (P-38L-1 44-24876) to serve with the 431st had been flown by Capt Edwin Weaver on the ill-fated 7 January 1945 mission that saw Maj McGuire killed in action. *Doots II* had the devil's head motif applied to its boom radiator in late April 1945.

27

P-38L-5 44-25482 of 1Lt Raymond H Werth, 431st FS, Lingayen, June 1945

1Lt Werth apparently joined the 431st FS soon after 1 January 1945, and took charge of *Irish ANGEL* sometime thereafter. Although he was vague about the reference for the name on the nose many years after the war, Werth remembered that it referred to someone he held in great esteem. The P-38 lasted until VJ-Day, although there is no mention of it in the group's December 1945 inventory list.

28

P-38L-5 44-25638 of 1Lt Louis D DuMontier, 431st FS, Lingayen, May 1945

1Lt Louis DuMontier was an old hand with the 431st by the time he received this aircraft, having claimed a 'Jack' on 27 November 1944 and two Zeros over Clark Field on Christmas Day. He had just parted company with his sweetheart when he was issued with 44-25638, but he still wanted to name his P-38 for the most important lady in his life. At that point in time it was his mother, and not wanting to incur derision from his comrades, he nicknamed his P-38 *MADU* – the name he had given his mother when he was a toddling infant!

29

P-38L-5 44-25635 of 2Lt R Werner, 431st FS, Lingayen, mid-1945

Werner was also one of the last wartime additions to the group, and little is recorded about him or his interestingly marked P-38. We can assume that he named his Lightning after his sweetheart, and that the Texas flag below the name denoted that he hailed from the Lone Star State.

30

P-38L-5 44-26778 of Flt Off Tony Paplia, 431st FS, Lingayen, summer 1945

Flt Off Tony Paplia was assigned to the 431st in April 1945, and he took charge of '138' after its previous pilot, Capt Bill Weaver, left the unit. Papia immediately changed the fighter's name from *Mrs. BILL* to *Winell* in honour of his girlfriend. Paplia still maintains a fondness for this P-38, having flown missions in the aircraft beyond VJ-Day.

31

P-38H-1 42-66682 of Capt John S Loisel, 432nd FS, Dobodura, January 1944

Loisel claimed as many as four of his eleven kills in this aircraft, which he christened *SCREAMIN' KID*. P-38s would typically survive less than six months in the frontline with V Fighter Command, but 42-66682 remained in service with the 475th FG for more than eight. Indeed, Loisel claimed his first kills with it as early as 15 October 1943 when he downed two 'Zekes' over Oro Bay. He continued to fly the aircraft until late January 1944, when the first of the vastly improved J-models arrived in the Solomons.

32

P-38L-5 44-25443 of Maj John S Loisel, 475th FG HQ, Dulag, January 1945

This aircraft was assigned to 475th FG ops officer Maj Loisel in January 1945, and he flew it for many months until he became CO of the group in July 1945. He may have claimed his final kill (a Ki-84) with the fighter on 28 March 1945.

33

P-38H-5 42-66817 of Capt Thomas B McGuire, 431st FS, Dobodura, December 1943

This particular P-38H-5 was McGuire's second Lightning, his first (H-1 42-66592) having been written off following damaged inflicted by enemy cannon fire during a dogfight near Wewak on 29 August 1943 – its pilot claimed a 'Zeke' and a 'Tony' destroyed in return. 42-66817 lasted until it was replaced by a new J-model in January 1944, McGuire having by then raised his tally to 16 confirmed kills.

34

P-38L-5 44-25600 of Maj Elliot Summer, 432nd FS, Lingayen, July 1945

This aircraft was the final mount of Elliot Summer, although by the time it was issued to him in early 1945 he had claimed all of his victories. The fighter was unusual in that it boasted the 432nd FS's emblem on its nose, along with the more standard CO's stripes and yellow unit markings. 44-25600's brief reign as the CO's mount ended when Summer rotated home in July 1945. Just a matter of days later, on 20 July, the fighter was lost on a training flight when its pilot, 2Lt Frazee, suffered complete electrical failure and was forced to bale out.

35

Ki-43-II KAI 'Oscar', ex-77th Sentai, Hollandia, April 1944

This airworthy Ki-43 was found abandoned at Hollandia following the Allied invasion in April 1944. The fighter had almost certainly been a part of the 77th Sentai prior to its capture. Stripped to bare metal and nicknamed *RACOON Special* (the call-sign of the 8th FS, which also flew it), the aircraft was test flown by P-38 pilots from the 432nd FS. Fifth Air Force records hint that the agile Nakajima fighter may have been sent back to the USA for more thorough testing.

36

P-38L-1 (serial unknown) of 1Lt John A Tilley, 431st FS, Clark Field, April 1945

Tilley shared the number '116' with another pilot when he joined the 475th FG late in 1943. Sometime in 1944 he took sole ownership of '116', and received the P-38L that became *Bette Ann* in late 1944 on Leyte Island. His final kill was scored on 26 December 1944 (an A6M5 Zero) in this Lightning. He was often a reluctant wingman to the demanding Maj Tom McGuire during the Philippines campaign.

UNIT HERALDRY

1

475th Fighter Group

It is not certain who designed the group emblem, but it first began to appear on camp signs during the final months of the war. It is possible that the lightning bolt on a crossbow, superimposed on a blue shield, was drawn by 431st FS groundcrewman George Jeschke, who did most of the squadron's nose art, as well as other drawings. The emblem itself has a possible internal device in the arrangement of the stars around the crossbow. Four of the stars have seven points while one has five, thus providing a visual reference to four-seven-five. This emblem, and the motto *In Proelio Guadete* (be joyful in battle), were finally approved by the USAF in1956.

2

431st Fighter Squadron

The devil's head emblem is generally attributed to ace John Tilley, who flew with the squadron practically from its formation. The unit call-sign 'Hades' lent itself to the 431st, and then the entire group, being dubbed 'Satan's Angels'. Whenever the demon head is shown independently, it

features a golden halo as well as the stars of the Southern Cross. This emblem was approved in 1944, and remained virtually intact throughout the squadron's history.

3

432nd Fighter Squadron

1Lt Henry Toll was credited with designing the original 'Clover' emblem depicting 'Uncle Sam' riding a lightning bolt over a four-leaf clover, superimposed on a yellow diamond. This historic design was changed after the war to an eagle talon grasping a lightning bolt on a black disc, edged in gold.

4

433rd Fighter Squadron

Nobody takes credit for the outlandish blue demon on a white cloud brandishing a blazing machine gun, with lightning bolts projecting from his evil eyes. The figure probably emanates from the original sobriquet adopted by the unit – 'The Fighting Blue Devils'. In 1954, the squadron adopted a new emblem in line with the 'Satan's Angels' motif of the 431st FIS.

INDEX